LOVE SEES DIFFERENTLY

LETTING GO OF OUR MISSION, EMBRACING HIS

JOEY LETOURNEAU

DEDICATION

To: One Child Campaign

Your mission is not only a powerful demonstration of God's love, but a growing testimony that multiplies further than eyes can see—because of "Who" you are. Thank you for living out Love's perspective, and empowering many others to live the same.

TABLE OF CONTENTS

ACKNOWLEDGMENTS

Dad & Mom: You paved the way for our calling in mission as we seek to join God in His.

Jackie: Your encouragement towards the need for this book is a huge reason it has come to fruition.

Caleb: Without your prayers and support, partnership, and most of all your friendship, this book wouldn't have been possible.

Martha Robbins: Thank you for your editing expertise. You helped bring out the best in this project.

To our incredible prayer partners and supporters: Thank you for empowering us in this journey of learning to join God in mission.

Destiny: Because nothing I am privileged to write is possible without you!

Father, God: You have Fathered me, fed me, and led me straight from your heart, and by Your voice. I am dependent on You in the most joyous ways. I hope that never lessens, and always grows. I love you!

INTRODUCTION:

JOHN 5:19

Then Jesus answered and said to them, "Most assuredly, I say to you, the Son can do nothing of Himself, but what He sees the Father do; for whatever He does, the Son also does in a like manner."

Whether we were joining part of a trip, welcoming a mission team, taking our own trips, or embracing daily opportunities to love on those around us while living in Ethiopia, I have always heard one question tied to mission repeated over and again. If you've asked this question, it's okay; we all have. This particular question is a standard, expected query that is nothing less than normal. It's natural, cultural even. It's a question I have asked too many times myself. But just because the question might be seen as the norm doesn't mean it is the right question. The goal here isn't so much to focus on what not to ask, but perhaps, what we *could* be asking first, as well as of Whom we are inquiring most.

Mission leaders everywhere concentrate on having this question answered before it can even be asked. Eager hearts are searching for purpose, and they hope this query will begin to reveal such. Experts study tirelessly for the pertinent information that will

1

back up the answer, and all of us look to make the answer our own. The question is one of noble intent and responsible planning, and is used by wonderful people everywhere. But I still can't help but wonder if we've allowed a cultural standard to replace some of what we *could* be asking.

"What are we going to be doing?" This is the inquiry that shapes our lives and mission everywhere, integral to mission's procedural requirements. It sounds so simple and harmless. And while it isn't harmful in intent, I still have to wonder if it could be robbing us of a better way. After all, good is often the worst enemy of best. And while our culture of mission is very good, I have to dig deeper and question whether our culture of mission could in fact be watering down God's ideas or hopes in mission. I have to challenge the perspective I have adopted and inquire of something—Someone—more. I have to move from wondering what *I* will be doing and begin to question something greater: *Could I be missing out on what God is doing?*

If we open the eyes of our hearts we will see God, Love Himself, as being more present in our moment, and our mission, than we ever imagined. In that moment we have an opportunity, before we jump into our own well-meaning agenda, when we can silence *our* question long enough to listen and hear *His*. *"Do you know what I AM doing?"* God asks us. Perhaps He aches while desiring to be part of our mission, wondering as loud as any of us will listen, *"Are you too busy with the way you want to build My kingdom to quiet your heart, take a little time with Me, and inquire of the unique way I AM moving in the place or person in front of you?"*

We have plans, programs, processes and agenda for each outreach, every mission and for nations everywhere. I'm thankful for these missions. These aren't bad things at all, but are our culturally approved ways the best available? To be honest, I'm not trying to convince you of my way of doing mission. In fact, I don't think there is any one "best way" to do mission. The way isn't a method, but a Person. God still very much uses these plans and efforts of ours whether they are His intended ways or not, and He gently corrals us over time back into His best version as much as we will allow. That's just Who God is, always using His love and grace to see His strength be made perfect in our weakness (2 Corinthians 12:9). And from personal experience, I'm very grateful for that! I've needed that corralling more than once—and probably much more than I know.

We have to acknowledge that God is doing much more in a nation, a community or a person than what we can ever plan for. He is an excited Father, to us and to those we are reaching, waiting to surprise us and blow our plans away! His grace is sufficient to invade and use all our grand, well-meaning plans whether we have truly inquired of Him or not. But His strength is made most perfect when we admit our weakness beforehand—when we can say, "I don't know," and make it our primary plan to actively stay in close enough proximity and alignment with God to listen to the One Who does know. Why? Because Love sees differently than we do. We think we want to see incredible fruit and impact? The Father wants to use us even more than we could hope for. But we have to learn to see the moment and the mission the way He does. We may want to solve someone's poverty, but what if He has a different, unlikely way, or a greater purpose He wants to accomplish? Maybe He wants to do more than we give Him credit for. Our goal must be *"to know the love of Christ which passes knowledge; that [we] may be filled with all the fullness of God,"* and to remember that He *"is able to do exceedingly abundantly above all that we ask or think, according to the power that works in us." (Ephesians 3:19-20)*

Maybe we're not supposed to have the answers, and maybe that's okay. Maybe we are simply called to be willing, surrendered and willing to fight against all compromise. To have nothing less for those we are engaging than to know the love of Christ that *surpasses all our knowledge*, and to be filled not just with the greatest love we can give them, but with the *fullness* that God so deeply wants them to know and receive. He is able to reveal something through us far greater than we've known before, constantly growing us and shattering any limits we may unknowingly place upon Him. *That's growth!* Growth isn't just learning with our mind—it's allowing the Father's territory in our heart to expand, to realize He's better than we've ever known or imagined. He will teach us things that we don't even know how to ask for! But it's up to us to let Him.

Chances are, our version of mission would then change, and we don't all like change all the time, do we? But it will only get better as we learn to trust His ways—exponentially better. After we know what He is doing and how He is moving, then we might truly discover what it is that we also will be doing, and how our dreams and hopes of purpose and impact will be re-shaped for the better within His. The Father beckons us to align our ways of mission with His; He is waiting for the day that we, like His Son, will look up with the eyes of our hearts firmly fixed on His unseen, surrounding presence and say: *"Father, what are You doing, and how can I join You?"* He is waiting for our love, like His, to see differently, and to allow for our mission to be lived out differently as well. We may be able to grow some fruit doing it our way, all the while giving Him the honor and glory. But in this "abiding" form of doing missions *with* our living God, we'll operate from a place perhaps less glamorous or less understood, with maybe fewer answers of our own, but we can trust Him that we will always be bearing an impossible sort of fruit—fruit that remains! (John 15)

> *Then Jesus answered and said to them, "Most assuredly, I say to you, the Son can do nothing of Himself, but what He sees the Father do; for whatever He does, the Son also does in a like manner." (John 5:19)*

Whether involved in direct ministry, a mission trip, or the daily routines of life, my family has adopted this verse as our personal way of mission. It was first embedded in me as I worked with my supervisor, who was the Global Prayer Director at Youth for Christ International, to form what would be my job description. Not only was it a personal verse, it became a "professional" verse, if I could even refer to mission as such. It was the summation of my job—to see what God was doing, join Him and empower others to do the same.

Jesus' words in this verse constantly chisel away at my agenda, reform my plans and redeem my hopes and dreams when they veer off track from being found within His. I am always re-learning just how much my Heavenly Father wants my life's purposes and calling to succeed, so much so that He won't let me settle for my often watered-down version. So, that's how I ask of Him now, praying He will never allow me to settle for anything less than His best. My best? It's not good enough; my experience and understanding are too limited. But the Father's best? Wow, only He can lead me there. And if Jesus, the Son of God, could do nothing of Himself but only what He saw the Father doing, how can we approach mission in any other way? John 5:19 helps us see mission through a new lens and let go of our agenda long enough not to miss out on how He is calling us to join Him in His.

Once, while traveling in Rwanda with my wife, Destiny, and our firstborn daughter, Mercy, God allowed us to see the possibilities in allowing these counter-cultural words of Jesus to come to life in us. We had been traveling the country roads of Rwanda for more than a week already, and on this particular day we were setting out for a bumpy ride of three to four hours each way to a local church where I would speak to a conference of young, emerging leaders.

It had been a long, tiring trip, but a great one at that! We had met so many incredible, local leaders whom God was raising up, the kind that give you such hope for the Father's plans for a nation. The leaders themselves said they felt they were "exploiting" us, as we had traveled and spoken multiple times each day. However, I wouldn't have traded the exhaustion for a thing. We saw God showing up in the big and the small. And I can't forget to mention that we also saw part of God's plan for us personally. On Sunday, just before this final trip to the young leaders' conference in the countryside, Mercy came to personally know and believe in Jesus as her Savior. It was a joyous surprise, as you can imagine. But God had even greater ideas He was covertly working on to turn our personal surprise into another, multiplied surprise of His own. The Father is good like that, when we let Him be. However, even when I learn that, I seem to have to re-learn it again.

Anyway, I was spent physically as the conference was starting and still asking the Lord what He wanted to do that day. But I couldn't get any clarity. So I continued in prayer as I awaited my turn at the microphone, continually giving the time and each person back to God. Once I began speaking I sensed the Holy Spirit really begin to move. He was bigger than the words I could offer, and the large group I was speaking to seemed to be locked in and really receiving. But then it happened—*the interruption.* Not all interruptions are bad when it comes to God's ways; sometimes, perhaps even most of the time, He is actually speaking through them and trying to get our attention.

We were at the climax of the message, with the young leaders on the edges of their seats, when approximately three hundred school children burst through the large, tin doors. You see, the church in which the conference was being held was literally planted on a local, rural school property. Pretty strategic actually! We all turned to see the kids, though we probably didn't have to as we could already hear them quite well. Imagine the scene of three hundred elementary students flooding into an "adults focused" meeting. It could have been chaotic! Instead, amidst the clamor, I quieted my heart and just asked, *"What are you doing, Lord?"* My heart sensed His answer clearly and immediately. I was to stop everything I was doing because the Father wanted to focus on His kids, in His way. And little did we know, He had already set us up and prepared us for His purposes the previous day.

As I waited for the kids to join us and come sit near the front, Destiny, who was sitting about ten feet behind me, called out gently, "Remember what God did yesterday with Mercy." God had clearly begun to let her in on our new plan now, too. So I invited Mercy up to stand with me as I began to address the children. We stopped the current message entirely and simply began to speak to the kids about Jesus, Who was clearly present and knocking on the doors of their hearts. I gave Mercy, who was only four years old, the microphone so she could speak to them with the few words of their local language she had been learning. Having Mercy speak broke down all the walls between us. They connected to a childlike innocence, with Mercy's presence making Jesus that much more real for them. Our translator was doing an incredible job facilitating and clearly had a huge heart for the kids himself.

After Mercy's greetings, I followed Destiny's suggestion and began to let them in on what had happened in Mercy's life just the day before. Testimonies speak so loudly, much more so than the most eloquent words. It gave the kids the chance to stare at the fingerprints of Jesus on Mercy's life and imagine those same hands lovingly embracing them too.

Then, we asked the kids if they wanted to know Jesus, too. Their hearts were ripe, more than we could have imagined. It's why God sent them to us that day. He had already been moving in their lives, just the same way He had prepared Mercy, and us, the day before. I'm not big on numbers at all; rarely do I ever keep track of ministry "results" whatsoever. But for the sake of showing the difference between what God wanted to do versus what we were doing, you've got to know that roughly two hundred kids of the three hundred came forward to connect with Jesus that day.

God spoke to us that day through the interruption, and thankfully it was a loud enough interruption for us to take notice. Sometimes it can be much more subtle. Sometimes He is patiently waiting next to one unlikely soul who was far off from our original plan or agenda. Sometimes He is whispering while we continue to talk or go about our "adult" programs. Sometimes we are looking for mission and purpose so much that we miss out on the purposes and plans that He has already prepared and laid out for us to join Him in. But I think most often He is waiting for us to echo the words and actions of His Son, Jesus: ***"Most assuredly, I say to you, the Son can do nothing of Himself, but what He sees the Father do; for whatever He does, the Son also does in a like manner."***

God most certainly knows what *our* plans are and what we are doing. But what He asks is this: *"Can you see what I AM doing?*

Are you ready to join Me in something even better?" It's not the first time He's asked. And thankfully it won't be the last.

> **"Behold, I will do a new thing, now it shall spring forth; shall you not know it?" (Isaiah 43:19)**

Love sees differently than we do. As we give Him our ways, He'll show us His.

CHAPTER 1:

SURRENDER IN MISSION

Part 1: Trusting God or Man

"For this cause I have raised thee up, for to show in thee My power."

—Andrew Murray, *Absolute Surrender*[1]

It is easy to try to find our own worth in mission, or to prove our worth through mission. Yet God calls us not to prove what we are, but to show Who He is through our surrender to Him. Surrender makes room in our lives for God to be seen for the loving, faithful Father He is. Our works can honor Him, but His ways operating through our lives will always reveal Him.

And the Lord said to Gideon, "The people who are with you are too many for Me to give the Midianites into their hands, lest Israel claim glory for itself against Me, saying, 'My own hand has saved me.'

"Now, therefore, proclaim in the hearing of the people saying, 'Whoever is fearful and afraid, let him turn and depart at once from Mount Gilead.'" And twenty-two thousand of the people returned, and ten thousand remained.

But the Lord said to Gideon, "The people are still too many; bring them down to the water, and I will test them for you there. Then it will be, that of whom I say to you, 'This one shall go with you,' the same shall go with you; and of whomever I say to you, 'This one shall not go with you,' the same shall not go."

So he brought the people down to the water. And the Lord said to Gideon, "Everyone who laps from the water with his tongue, as a dog laps, you shall set apart by himself; likewise everyone who gets down on his knees to drink."

And the number of those who lapped, putting their hand to their mouth, was three hundred men; but all the rest of the people got down on their knees to drink water.

Then the Lord said to Gideon, "By the three hundred men who lapped I will save you, and deliver the Midianites into your hand. Let all the other people go, every man to his place." (Judges 7:2-7)

Now, I have to be careful not to let familiarity rob the little layers of power from within this story, which familiarity often likes to do. See, Gideon was on a mission—a direction commissioned by God—and yet, clearly, Gideon did not go about this mission in the way he would have probably expected, nor in the way he likely would have chosen on his own. God had greater purposes in mind, far beyond just accomplishing victory and establishing the promise that He'd given Gideon regarding the Midianites. God accomplished Gideon's mission far differently than any of us would strategize or plan. And the only way He was able to do so was by having a leader who was still willing to be led, one who was devoted to surrendering His will and ways to join the Father in how He was moving.

Our version of victory is easy for God, but He is looking far beyond what we see as victory. He is looking beyond just winning the battle and handing the promise into our hands. He cares too much about all the people caught in the process. He wants His nature to be known, seen, felt. We might see victory as a prayer prayed or a young man fed, but God wants to do that, and more! God wants to reveal Himself, to show Who He is—and to do so, He uses people like you and me, like Gideon. He looks for those vessels who are surrendered, and therefore empty enough of their own knowledge and strengths; those who've gotten rid of the water in their vessel so that it doesn't rob Him of the oil that He wants to pour out instead.

Gideon made himself empty, not in a self-depreciating way, but in a surrendered, believing fashion. He trusted God enough to surrender his own ideas, and even most of his own men who were prepared for battle. Can you imagine what Gideon might have been thinking? How would you respond? It's easy now, knowing Gideon's story, to say that we would be obedient no matter what we were asked, regardless of what common sense we had to surrender. But would we not be worried about what others thought? Would we not be afraid of appearing as a fool, or over confident when sending our troops away? Would we not reason to ourselves that this wasn't God speaking to us, and that we should just go the safe route with what makes more sense? I'm not talking about trying to break the box and do crazy things for God. I'm simply talking about mission that doesn't conform to common sense and human reasoning. This doesn't stem from trying to be different, but by being so surrendered that we lose ourselves in loving obedience, trusting that His ways will prove better, and deeper, in the long run. Not only must this have seemed to Gideon and his troops like a counter-intuitive strategy for victory, one could also say it was a pretty unique and humbling process that God chose while trying to whittle down that army to the three hundred He planned to use. Surrender and true humility require us to not care what others think in order to be fully engaged with the Father and His ways.

From Gideon's perspective, or even according to our own expectations, people or at least the number of them may have appeared to be the means for victory. So what was it that God asked Gideon to surrender to Him? People. Gideon had to surrender to God his own potentially well-conceived purposes and plans for battle and trust God's unique ways instead. Not only that, but he had to surrender the very people who would have carried out his strategies. That's a lot of surrender for a battle in which your life is potentially on the line. But it also shows us that "surrender" wasn't just a requirement or lesson God had for Gideon. We tend to see surrender in the vein of sacrifice, and see it as a test we must pass—*but it is so much more!* Surrender was actually God's strategy for seeing His mission come about fully. Surrender became the Israelites' strength, not because it added anything to them, but simply because it aligned them with how God was moving.

Ultimately, surrender proved to be the best mission Gideon could employ. God asked him to surrender his plans, and He asked him to surrender his people. God wasn't calling Gideon to weakness; He was empowering him to walk in a different, but higher strength. So often, we associate surrender with a negative connotation. But through God's eyes, surrender isn't a retreat; rather, the kingdom demonstrates surrender to be an offensive step forward into the beautiful purposes God waits for us to discover with Him. Surrender will lead us, side by side with Jesus, to the greatest fruit there is to be found in any mission. Surrender removes fear, because the enemy can't steal—or scare you with the thought of losing—that which you have already surrendered. Surrender frees us from insecurity and welcomes us into a form of mission that may not be typical but is of the utmost purity in its form. Why? Because there is nothing left of self to drive us or pollute the possibilities or the people we encounter. All we have left is what God pours through the powerfully yielded emptiness of our lives, which in kingdom terms ends up making us and others exceedingly, and abundantly, full. (See Ephesians 3:20.)

"For as the heavens are higher than the earth, so are My ways higher than your ways, and My thoughts than your thoughts. For as the rain comes down, and the snow from heaven, and do not return there, but water the earth, and make it bring forth and bud, that it may give seed to the sower and bread to the eater, so shall My word be that goes forth from My mouth; it shall not return to Me void, but it shall accomplish what I please, and it shall prosper in the thing for which I sent it." (Isaiah 55: 9-11)

This is a passage that constantly governs my thoughts, choices and life as a whole. It's the very foundation of our confidence in surrendering to God, and the reason that surrender is such a powerfully effective means for mission. Gideon couldn't have joined the Lord so easily in the testimony we now record if he didn't live out of this belief about God and His nature with every beat of his heart. It's one thing to speak this promise, or to acknowledge it as true and claim belief—*but do we really believe it?* I hope so, I really do. But if I honestly evaluate my actions, or the way I go about mission, do I reflect this verse? When "doing" mission do I put more trust in my plans and efforts, or in joining the Lord in His? Am I on a rescue mission, or my own journey with the Lord to carry out His mission? If we truly believe His ways and thoughts are higher than ours, it will be shown over and over again in our lives. If we really believe that His word does not return void, we would inquire of Him ALL THE TIME and wait to hear Him speak to us His fresh ways and strategies because we would know that otherwise it wouldn't work out to the best result possible. For me at least, this word tests the motives of my heart. Am I doing mission for me, to help me feel or look good, or am I genuinely stepping with Him into His purposes, where I know that His word and His mission will prosper every time? This verse is so popular, yet it is truly a call to surrender! And surrender isn't all that popular a method compared to other methods we're likely to pursue.

The ways of mission that we live out have the opportunity to be so much more potent if we will only trust God's ways above ours, if we will let go of our plans and trust Him to give them back to us in even better form than when we handed them over. Surrender truly opens our eyes because our surrender goes all in on God's higher perspective and allows us to join Him there, enabling us to see the lay of the land far better than from where we might stand. Surrender lifts us higher, like an elevator taking us to a new level and making us privy to what we couldn't see while still standing on the first level. The more we let go, the further we go with Him! And before you know it, we're looking down at the possibilities with Him, shaking our head and saying, "Oh, yeah, I'm glad I didn't go that direction. I didn't see it like that or realize what could happen." Or, "Wow, look how much fruit is just waiting to be found in that small hidden valley where no one can see!" Surrender gives us foresight and removes our need to strive for fruit, which is sometimes what we're afraid of. We feel that if we don't create the fruit, we might not get the credit! But the best fruit is rarely sown and reaped by the same person, at least if you listen to Jesus discuss such harvest in John 4. (We'll dive deeper into that subject later in the book.)

See, we're not just surrendering our ways of mission; we're also surrendering our right to do the sowing in our own personal greenhouse, and the reaping for the benefit of our own barn. Surrender can be scary like that, because as much as we say it's all for God's glory, even if that really is our heart, it can be hard to trust Him that heaven sees and knows when we really desire the recognition of man as well. Our fear of man, or need for approval, really is what keeps a verse like the one above from bridging the gap between our belief in God and our lifestyle of mission *with* God. Surrender demonstrates that our trust is in God, and not in what man thinks. It's not how we're taught to lead, but it's most certainly how Jesus led. For now, please remember this: The Father believes in you, so much so that your surrender only lets Him walk with you more, and to use you to purely pour His love through you to those He died to reach. If mission truly isn't about us, then surrender becomes our new favorite word.

Moving Forward:

1. If we search deep beyond the surface, we all have different motives for "doing" mission. What do you need to surrender that will free you to simply join God where He is moving?

2. Can you remember one time when your heart felt a unique, perhaps unlikely, conviction from the Lord to step in one way, but you felt compelled to join the majority or stay with the status quo in a more "normal" way?

3. Describe in your own words the hidden power of surrender.

Part 2: My #1 Priority

Here is where it gets personal, for me at least. God has used surrender in my life more often than I can remember, not for me to fear, but as a doorway into greater opportunities to join Him in His most joyous ways of mission. This hasn't always looked rewarding, and it certainly hasn't always been easy. Surrender has led me down paths of uncertainty, only to discover just how close He was each step of the way. It has required me to let go of that which I could have used to build for myself great reputation, or security for my family and me, and, instead, to trust Him that heaven's eyes carry more value than earth's. (Easier said than done, huh?) But surrender has also challenged my leadership, at times calling for me to lead in different ways—ways that might not be the norm or easy to follow. It has made me trust Him more than I trust my own leadership, learning to understand that my leadership is only as fruitful as the freshness of my real and close connection with Him. People want our attention, but we can't truly empower them if we do not first firmly affix our attention on God, what He is doing and how He is moving. Everything else then flows from there.

My favorite term for such leadership (I've described it in some of my other writing as well) is called: *First Love Leadership*. It is based on one of my life passages, Revelation 2:1-7, Jesus' words to the church at Ephesus. By the way, it's not my life verse because I have it figured out but because it must remain my fresh and daily pursuit, one that I hope never grows too familiar.

"To the angel of the church of Ephesus write, 'These things says He who holds the seven stars in His right hand, who walks in the midst of the seven golden lampstands: "I know your works, your labor, your patience, and that you cannot bear those who are evil.

And you have tested those who say they are apostles and are not, and have found them liars; and you have persevered and have patience, and have labored for My name's sake and have not become weary.

"Nevertheless I have this against you, that you have left your first love. Remember therefore from where you have fallen; repent and do the first works. . . . "'" (Revelation 2:1-5)

As many of us know, it's very easy to get swept up with "what we are doing" and the work we are doing *for* God, whether as a volunteer, in a ministry role or in some form of mission. This "love letter" from Jesus reminds us that He sees our diligence, our faithfulness and our good intentions. But He reminds us that this wasn't the place we started from. We didn't start with Him from a place of "doing"; we began our life with Jesus in a place of total "being," as in, back then, "I couldn't stop myself from being in total love with Him." It wasn't a journey born out of duty but rather out of that first love relationship that sparked our passion and eventually led us to where we are today.

Mission can typically make us even more dutiful; I mean, it's even in the name, right? We start to bear the responsibility or burdens of leadership, or "doing God's work." We start to take ourselves more seriously, which by the way only makes surrender all the more difficult. But I have to ask myself, what was it that put me in position to be seen as a leader in the first place? It wasn't my capabilities in doing God's work for Him; most likely, people saw me as a leader or as ready for a role in mission because my heart burned so passionately for Jesus that I was blazing forward, unable to get my eyes off Him! Such a time in your own life might have been long ago, but it was likely at the core of your journey. When you burn after Him like this, before you know it you find yourself perhaps a little separated from the pack and out ahead. Imagine this, if you would, and picture yourself, or someone else that has suddenly separated from the pack. Our normal reaction is to look at that person and deem them a leader. Why? They are leading by example rather than by title and have been found in a "position" of leadership, by distancing themselves from others in pursuit of a goal. They are leading because they are *following Jesus so hard, and wanting to be so close!* But guess what happens next? As soon as we call someone a leader, or they see themselves that way, a new expectation is birthed. Now the position becomes more about its title or expectations. Now said "leader" feels the need to turn around and face the people he or she is supposed to be leading. It's from the best intentions, of course, but as you can imagine, looking backward makes it a lot harder to keep your eyes on Jesus as your first love, and a lot harder to join Him where He is moving. Now, the leader is relegated to teaching and modeling the principles and plans learned up until that time, largely missing out on staying fresh with Him, where it is easier to recognize what He is doing and how to join Him. This is our typical expectation of leadership and the cycle that commonly follows. Do you see the challenge we face?

If I have turned to face the people in order to bear the responsibility of leadership, I'm no longer doing what put me there in the first place. It's really hard to join Jesus and follow so well when at least half your attention is now given to the people. It helps me understand why Paul would say, "Follow me as I follow Christ." He didn't say, "I'll teach you the way." He basically said, *"Hey, it's great you're here, but I have no clue myself if I don't keep my eyes, ears and heart glued to Jesus! No offense, but I'll follow Him, and you just follow that example until you catch up and can pursue Him closely for yourself."* Now those are words I want to echo with my walk. And really, they sound a lot like what Jesus stated in John 5:19: ***"Most assuredly, I say to you, the Son can do nothing of Himself, but what He sees the Father do; for whatever He does, the Son also does in a like manner."***

For me, that's First Love Leadership. That's how we can effectively lead others, and that's how I want to do mission. I know my own weakness, and the best thing I have going for me is to stay ever close to Him. I've got to surrender my expectations of myself, and the expectations of others. Often, we don't surrender because we fear that letting go could allow for mistakes or errors. However,

God will never lead us in an irresponsible way. If I am leading by being surrendered first to God, I can't say that I'm not stewarding my role well—I'm simply stewarding through trust in Him rather than in my own hands or abilities. I have to surrender my role, my responsibilities, my works and plans to whatever extent necessary to keep my eyes on Him. Otherwise, I'll be blazing my own noble path with a zeal that the Lord certainly appreciates, but it'll only be a matter of time before I need another one of those "love letters" calling me back to surrender all that and return to the way in which Jesus and I began together.

God led me through one example of First Love Leadership in a very specific way. I had just been brought on by Youth for Christ International (YFCI) as their Global Youth Prayer Coordinator. YFCI is in well over one hundred nations, so I easily could have felt a big burden of leadership and reasoned that I needed to work all the harder to be a faithful steward. But in trying to keep my eyes on my first love, I found God leading me through a different means.

I'll never forget standing in our apartment in Castle Rock, Colorado, asking God this question. *Lord, what is your #1 priority, besides my intimacy with You, for me to lead well in this role?* I waited quietly to see how God would direct me, whether it would be through a specific passage in the Word, an encouragement from someone else, or His still small voice in my heart. He spoke rather quickly, and this time, it was through the latter. The Holy Spirit nudged my heart with a picture of God's #1 role for me to lead well and handle this responsibility in His best ways. It was really simple. With spiritual eyes, I saw myself standing with arms stretched straight up in the air towards God, hands open in total surrender. That's what He wanted. That would be the #1 priority in order for me to move forward in this international leadership role—surrender. This wasn't exactly what I expected, nor is it what we typically put at the top of our job descriptions or priority list. But it was clear and convicting. God was asking me not to take the mission, the needs, the burdens, the role or anything else and try to bear them on my own. The Father wanted me to leave everything in His hands so that I could keep my eyes on Him rather than on the mission. He knew that I would likely work my way through my responsibilities out of noble intentions but missing out on His best, or I could surrender and trust Him to show me His higher ways, with each step forward.

Ever since that moment, I've received many nudges from Him reminding me of that priority of His. *"Give it back,"* He says, when I try to take it on myself. *"Hand it over,"* He nudges me, when I feel the heaviness getting to be too much. *"Give it here,"* He reminds me, when I start to make it more about me. And each time, He asks for me to start from the beginning, to surrender my ways of leading and instead return to simply loving Him. When I do, no matter how often He has to remind me, I re-discover that passionate pursuit and intimate alignment with Him that leads to more fruit than I could ever create on my own. I might not see it all right now, but He promises that it will come.

Moving Forward:

1. It's easy to say that God is our First Love. But what other good thing—like mission or leadership—is there in your life that you allow to compete for that spot?

2. What does First Love Leadership mean to you, and where God is taking your heart in this regard? What might His current love letter to you read like?

3. What does it mean to you for surrender to be your #1 priority in the mission God has called you to? Do you trust Him with that? Why is that trust challenging?

Part 3: Cross Mission vs. Carnal Mission

It seems impossible to me that we can declare our unrelenting belief in the power of the cross while at the same time fearing, or discounting, the power and need for surrender as a "go-to" strategy in our lives and mission. Now, I don't know that we actually consciously discount surrender; it's just that it usually takes a back seat to *our* wisdom. I'm a big fan of wisdom, but of God's wisdom more than my own.

> *And suddenly, one of those who were with Jesus stretched out his hand and drew his sword, struck the servant of the high priest, and cut off his ear. But Jesus said to him, "Put your sword in its place, for all who take the sword will perish by the sword. Or do you think that I cannot now pray to My Father, and He will provide Me with more than twelve legions of angels? How then could the Scriptures be fulfilled, that it must happen thus?" (Matthew 26:51-54)*

In this passage, Peter, such a close, revered follower of Jesus, reacted more according to natural common sense, wanting to take God's mission into his own hands. Peter was suddenly thrust into his own mission mindset. He was going to do the saving. He was going to be the faithful one who stood up by Jesus' side and did something about the terrible things about to happen. Peter was noble, missional, passionate, but he was also operating out of carnal thinking. He was trying to accomplish God's purposes through the best way He knew, but even our best is still merely man's way until we learn how God is moving in a specific time.

Peter's action left Jesus to reiterate His and the Father's plan to choose surrender instead, essentially saying: "No, Peter, that's man's way. There is something greater to be accomplished, and as crazy as it sounds, I've got to surrender to these men right now for My Father's true purposes to be fulfilled."

As wonderful a gift as wisdom is—and it is something we need to operate in each day—it is still a carnal way of thinking to expect yesterday's wisdom to sum up what God wants to do today. God is living, moving, breathing and leading us forward in new mission with Him all the time. We like to come up with processes and programs that work and that can easily be repeated, and many of them are wonderful ideas. But just because God did something one way one time doesn't mean that's the strategy He'll choose next time. Peter's response in that moment in Gethsemane was equivalent to the battles of the Old Testament. But Jesus was there to say, *"My Father is doing something new—do you not recognize it?"*

Peter was among the closest followers of Jesus. We're not talking about one of the Pharisees who wanted to do things the religious way; we're talking about a guy who had spent nearly every waking moment with Jesus during those years leading up to that conversation in the Garden of Gethsemane. Peter wasn't doing the wrong thing, but rather trying to do the right thing the wrong way. Peter was simply operating out of his own belief that he could bring about God's best plans through his own ways of thinking. God does want to use us, and use us powerfully. But He is looking for those who will first inquire of Him, who will surrender their "crusade" or mission and see what Love sees in the moment.

The power of surrender keeps us dependent on God's ways, always requiring that we hear Him fresh and new. The cross is the picture of Jesus stretching out His hands to the Father saying, **"Not My will, but Yours, be done" (Luke 22:42).** The cross was Jesus proving the powerful and effective strategy of surrender, defeating the enemy once and for all through one of the most unlikely plans ever—a plan surely not devised on earth. The cross was a new beginning, freeing us from our carnal nature and leading to Jesus being freshly and personally available to each of us every step of the way. The cross wasn't just a one-time act of victory, but an ongoing mission strategy.

That moment in Gethsemane wasn't the first time Peter questioned Jesus' plan of surrender, either. Peter did the same thing in Matthew 16:21-23 when Jesus predicted His death and resurrection. Do you remember Jesus' response that time? He said, *"Get behind Me, Satan! You are an offense to Me, for you are not mindful of the things of God, but the things of men."*

That's some strong language, certainly not the kind I want to receive from the Lord. But, Jesus wasn't condemning Peter, He was condemning the carnal way of thinking that Peter was applying to kingdom mission and calling. Again, Peter was ready to rush in with an answer that Jesus already had. Jesus knew He couldn't start applying reason or emotion to the Father's plans, diluting and separating God's oil with man's water. Surrender allows us to empty our vessel and make room for the oil God will pour out. It's not that any of us are trying to stray and do things "my" way or through self; Peter wasn't doing this consciously either. But we can be all too prone to trying to finish in the flesh what was begun in the Spirit. We can be prone to using drywall and insulation to build God's house and kingdom. The following verse is one that I'm often challenged by—challenged to return to the purity of trusting His unseen ways over my own well-reasoned ones.

Are you so foolish? Having begun in the Spirit, are you now being made perfect by the flesh? (Galatians 3:3)

I don't know about you, but that one stings a little! My brain can't even remember the number of times my heart knows that verse has been true for me. It's why we must continually ask God to renew our minds to His ways of mission before trying to take a valiant step like Peter. Sometimes, we just have to surrender. It might only be stepping back from an opportune moment for five minutes to ask God's perspective. It might mean stepping forward in love in a unique or uncomfortable way. It might even mean stepping back from a mission that "self" is drawn to, and let surrender show us a different way in which God is pulling us.

Just a couple years ago we had to make a huge surrender in the mission God called us to, trusting Him with the opinion of those watching, and believing that even though it appeared as a step backwards in the natural, God was going to use it for a giant leap forward in the long run.

While living in Ethiopia we spent a good bit of our time caring for and empowering kids from the street. At the same time, we worked with young, local leaders, training them and raising them up to take over this mission, and empowering them into their own. Eventually, just before we left, we opened a boys' street shelter where the kids could live and be cared for and empowered by these young leaders (spiritual fathers & mothers as we called them) in a variety of ways. Once it was time for us to move away from Ethiopia, we handed it all over to the local leaders and began to transition the ministry into their hands. This isn't the surrender I was speaking of; however, it is one more model of how we must look not only to "do" mission, but how to empower others in their purpose and calling. However, we'll discuss that further later on in the book.

We moved back to the U.S. and stayed in communication with the team and how they were leading the kids, the movement and at the shelter. There were definitely some growing pains, but the right steps forward aren't always easy at the outset. For the next two years, we still helped direct and oversee the leaders on big-picture decisions. But there came a time when a number of struggles were building up for the team and the shelter, and we were receiving e-mail after e-mail about the needs and how we needed to fix them, find more support, etc. I felt pressure to meet these needs, and I knew there were many eyes watching. However, as I prayed I felt like God showed me a bigger problem at the root of all the individual issues. We couldn't just put bandages on all the issues or else we would have become a spiritual nurse to needs that required something much deeper. God had a different strategy, and once again He showed me, and others who were praying with us, what can happen through the power of surrender.

God showed us that the current facility for the kids was too big—the whole operation was too unwieldy for the leadership structure and the direction God was leading. We usually think getting bigger demonstrates more fruit, but God wanted us to get smaller in order to grow and send out in different ways. We felt like we were supposed to surrender the facility and trust God for something else; however, we had no idea what or where that was.

When we first mentioned this to our local leaders, it didn't make sense to them. They listed all the facts, showing us why this shelter was needed and all the problems giving it up might cause. They were afraid of losing the ministry. Also, we knew there were others watching who might not understand and who could see the closing of the shelter as failure. However, God was asking us to surrender not just the shelter and our ministry, He was asking us to surrender our carnal ways of thinking and how we might apply our reasoning to His greater purposes. We had to trust that He cared about those kids, about the team of leaders and about us, even more than we did. And, we had to trust that He had a better outcome in mind than what we could hope for ourselves. So we closed the shelter while believing it was a step forward with God.

This was a nerve-wracking decision to make. What if it didn't work out? What if we never got things re-opened? What might happen to the kids during this time of limbo? How would the leadership team respond? What would people think of us? Those are the questions we often have to surrender, and instead, simply put our eyes back on Jesus and say, *"I trust You. I won't look at the circumstances and let them dictate my response; I'm going to look only at You, Lord, and trust that You see the circumstances better than I do. I'm going to trust Your eyes instead of my own."* Sounds pretty, but it doesn't always feel so pretty in the process.

We were amazed to see God not only answer our questions, but use this step back as a way to meet all the current needs and re-establish the mission. The provision that had been so scarce before suddenly flowed in, like a dam had been broken. The still-involved leaders rallied together in a new way, and it actually caused them to take greater ownership and sharpen their focus regarding how to move forward. We were so proud of how they responded to those circumstances. They grew, and so did the kids! Ever since then they have taken the ministry at the shelter as well as with the kids and made it their own. Because of surrender, which at first had been very uncomfortable, they were privileged to see God show up in the places where man removed his hands. Sometimes it is our own hands or perspective that can block what Love Himself really wants to do. But when we let go, we embrace God while He embraces—more powerfully and more beautifully—who, or what, we were trying to hold onto.

Jesus twice rejected Peter's advice on finishing His mission, instead choosing surrender and an unlikely route to join the Father. Why? Because Love sees differently than we do. I'm sure we all today are thankful He chose what our minds might not have chosen. Jesus used His surrender on the cross to bring about the greatest victory this world will ever know: He made Himself of no reputation, instead taking the form of a servant (Philippians 2:7). Our call to carry our cross each day is not a call to embrace mission as if He needs us to save the world; rather, it is our call to surrender in order to embrace mission the way Jesus did, as a servant. We are not just serving the people or needs we might encounter; first, we are serving the Father, and His purposes. His kind of mission isn't nearly as popular or trendy to the average eye, but its impact is one of perpetual fruit and heavenly gain.

Moving Forward:

1. Why is it so easy for us to respond out of carnal thinking, like Peter? How do you battle this in your own life and mission?

2. What is the difference between "carnal" thinking and "cross" thinking? How do these strategies differ?

3. Mission often validates something inside us that feels good. But most of Jesus' life and mission was incredibly misunderstood—not just by the world, but also by well-meaning leaders who thought they knew best. What if Jesus invited you on a mission that you knew was right, but that might leave you misunderstood in your obedience? How would you respond?

Part 4: Sacrifice or Multiplication?

The story of Abraham, Isaac, Mt. Moriah and everything that went on before and after is one of my favorite stories in the Bible. Why? Because in Abraham, we see someone who went against the grain, with God, without compromise and who watched God show up and reveal how kingdom thinking and living really works. To our mind, sacrifice doesn't always add up. But with God, it always multiplies.

> *Now it came to pass after these things that God tested Abraham, and said to him, "Abraham!" And he said, "Here I am." Then He said, "Take now your son, your only son Isaac, whom you love, and go to the land of Moriah, and offer him there as a burnt offering on one of the mountains of which I shall tell you." (Genesis 22:1-2)*

I love what Mt. Moriah represents. Though it is obviously a very famous site, it tends also to be most remembered, especially regarding Abraham, as a place of sacrifice and testing—where Abraham went to sacrifice his only, promised son, Isaac. However, that's where I differ with common thinking. I don't see Moriah just as a place of sacrifice; rather, I believe it is a place of multiplication—wild, organic, unstoppable, multiplication to grow God's family—if we'll trust Him.

> *Then on the third day Abraham lifted his eyes and saw the place afar off. And Abraham said to his young men, "Stay here with the donkey; the lad and I will go yonder and worship, and we will come back to you." So Abraham took the wood of the burnt offering and laid it on Isaac*

his son; and he took the fire in his hand, and a knife, and the two of them went together. (Genesis 22:4-6)

And Abraham stretched out his hand and took the knife to slay his son. (Genesis 22:10)

The following is an excerpt from chapter 5, "Offense vs. Defense," from one of my previous books, *The Life Giver*. It dives a little further into Abraham's trust of God and how his surrender of a wonderful gift like Isaac turned into widespread multiplication on top of Mt. Moriah that day.

Abraham had already left all to follow God. He had believed God at His word with far less than we have today. And God had accounted it to him for righteousness. Then, just when it seemed that Abraham's promise land had come to fruition, God tested and strengthened Abraham yet again.

The promise of Isaac had come forward in Abraham and Sarah's life—an impossible promise nevertheless. And now, God challenged Abraham's heart by asking him to give it back and trust Him with such blind faith in God's perfect love that he would put his son, his answered promise, on the altar.

This was a strategic moment for Abraham and creation as a whole. When God begins something new, He is going to see it all the way through, far beyond what we can see in that moment. God knew He could use Abraham to restart His offensive move and rebirth His family on earth, but He wouldn't allow Abraham into that position as a life-giver without knowing Abraham would not, could not, be moved. Not even by a lifelong dream or promise.

Abraham trusted in God's perfect, impenetrable love so much that he did not even feel the need to play defense when his own son actually was on the verge of being lost.

Abraham was so focused on the offensive assignment God had called him to that he could see beyond loss and prophetically grasp the victory of God.

Our youngest daughter has the middle name of Moriah. It has always been a special name to me because I believe Moriah is a place where multiplication of life begins. Moriah is the place where we are just starting to taste God's promise and the Lord gives us the option of doing us one better. He gives us an offer of obedience. He asks us to trust Him enough not to need to protect His promise. He asks us to entrust it back to Him knowing His perfect love for us removes the risk of loss and guarantees greater gain and multiplication. He challenges our motives to purify us. Are we in it for us or for Him? On Moriah, God is asking us what is in our hearts and what or who are we truly seeking. All the while, God has the love of an all-knowing Father. Behind His back, He has the promise in hand, ten-fold! That's the kind of abundant Father we are loved by.[2]

But the Angel of the Lord called to him from heaven and said, "Abraham, Abraham!" So he said, "Here I am." And He said, "Do not lay your hand on the lad, or do anything to him; for now I know that you fear God, since you have not withheld your son, your only son, from Me."

Then Abraham lifted his eyes and looked, and there behind him was a ram caught in a thicket by its horns. So Abraham went and took the ram, and offered it up for a burnt offering instead of his son. And Abraham called the name of the place, The-Lord-Will-Provide; as it is said to this day, "In the Mount of the Lord it shall be provided." (Genesis 22:11-14)

"By Myself I have sworn, says the Lord, because you have done this thing, and have not withheld your son, your only son—blessing I will bless you, and multiplying I will multiply your descendants as the stars of heaven and as the sand which is on the seashore. . . ." (Genesis 22:16-17)

Often what feels to us like a "sacrifice kind" of surrender is actually a "multiplication kind" of surrender as we partner with God. When we give Him back our promises, our purposes, our agendas and dreams, He knows He can trust us with the greater multiplication of fruit that He actually wants to accomplish through us. Abraham's version of provision there on Mt. Moriah may have been simply to keep his treasured son, Isaac. But God's form of provision was not only to provide for Isaac's life, but also to grow his life into as many descendants as the stars in the sky and the sand on the seashore.

God is a good, loving, abundant Father. His plans for us and for mission through us are exceedingly and abundantly beyond what we could ask or think. Mt. Moriah is not a place to be avoided when God calls our name to take that journey up, or when He asks us to put our mission or our identity on the line. It is the place where we get to know Him as the perfectly loving Father that He is and trust Him to take our greatest desires and multiply them beyond what we can count. *That's how good our Father is!*

How many kids might you run across that you'd love to rescue? I've had that thought and desire more than once, that's for sure. But we are not necessarily what they need. They need someone who will hold them, love them, but also put them back into the Father's hands where He can bring about His best, far beyond what we can still do with them in our arms. When we surrender in this way He will show us how to join Him in their lives. And chances are, He will multiply their lives and purpose far beyond even our best intentions.

The mission we will accomplish with God on His mount of surrender is more far reaching than any amount of work we can do according to our own plans on His behalf. It all comes down to where we place our trust. All in all, through trust, surrender stands to be one of the most powerful possibilities God has given us. Surrender is not just what we give up to start mission, it's a strategy God uses during mission to take our willingness and multiply it not just as far as our eyes can see, but as far as His do.

Surrender is waiting to be grabbed hold of, but our willingness to embrace the opportunity all depends on how we *see* it.

Moving Forward:

1. How have you allowed the negative connotation of "sacrifice" to keep you from taking advantage of the potential power of surrender? What if we anticipated multiplication instead of subtraction?

2. How you view God largely affects your view of surrender. How does your view of surrender change the more you see God as the good, loving Father that He is? Can you trust Him to always do you one better? Why? How?

3. How can you apply surrender to your life and calling? Is there something you've been holding back, protecting, that God actually wants to use for increase if put in His hands?

End Notes:

1. Andrew Murray, *Absolute Surrender* (London & Edinburgh: Marshall, Morgan & Scott, LTD., 1939), p. 57.
2. Joey LeTourneau, *The Life Giver* (Shippensburg, PA: Destiny Image Publishers, 2012) pp. 117-119.

CHAPTER 2:

THE FATHER IN MISSION

Part 1: The Father's Perspective

> *. . . In the presence of Him whom [Abraham] believed—*
> *God, who gives life to the dead and calls things*
> *which do not exist as though they did; who, contrary to*
> *hope, in hope believed, so that he became the father of*
> *many nations. . . . (Romans 4:17-18)*

To me, this verse demonstrates the transformational possibilities available to us when we see people, life and mission through the Father's eyes. He sees the people we are reaching out to differently than we do. We must do mission according to how He sees people, not how we see them. We often see them as projects, but the Father sees them as His kids—He sees family, and that's how we must love them, like family. That's what I love about God's promise to Abraham! God calls us family even before we know we are family. He calls us His kids even before we believe He's our Father. Just like it says, God calls that which doesn't exist as though it already did, just like He did in making Abraham a father of many nations. That's the power of God's perspective; we get to see His amazing possibilities and call them into existence with Him. We often see those we're reaching out to as broken, as lost or unsaved, as widow or orphan; but God is a Father, and He already sees each one as family. What if we reached out to people through that very same perspective? What if we didn't just attempt to meet their need or fill in their gaps—because we understood that mission is not merely a goodwill tour for spreading good news, but a worldwide family inviting each person to know they have already been included, according to the Father's love, in what has been finished through Jesus Christ? What if we saw with a greater vision that goes beyond the ministry we are "doing," and instead helped to reveal to people a Father who already sees them as *belonging*?

When we relate to those we encounter in mission, we must relate to them not according to what we see, nor according to their outward need or circumstance. We must see through the eyes of the Father, for He knows each of those needs as well as the deeper, further-reaching possibilities. Our eyes will often cause us to react to need, trying to fill a gap with what we have in our hands. God's eyes see deeper, further, and recognize possibilities that we do not. Living by His perspective will allow us to love not by what we have in our hands, but by what the Father has in His.

If you are a father or mother, you can probably understand this very well. As a father or mother you are going to relate to your children differently than anyone else will. You are going to see more hope, more potential, and have more belief and a different kind of love than anyone else, sometimes even to an irrational extent. Am I right? Why? Because no one else has the same perspective of your kids as you do. You may hire a babysitter for a couple hours, maybe even a couple days—and they might just do a wonderful job of caring for your kids. But they can't love them the way you do or make their love palatable to your kids unless they truly see and live towards your kids from your parental perspective. Perspective on the inside changes the very ways we naturally operate and respond on the outside. That's why the Father's perspective is *so vital* to mission *with* the Lord.

Do we truly realize how important God's kids are to Him, how special each and every one of them is in their own unique way? What would happen if, when on a mission trip, a local outreach or simply encountering someone in your daily routine, you in that moment put the Father in your place? How would He see this person? How would He respond? His love is not a frivolous love, but a deeply resonating, patient, always believing, relentless sort of love that goes far beyond the moment. To Him, this individual in front of you is not ministry; he or she is family! *He or she is His child!*

To the Father, the one we may call "lost" or "unsaved" *already belongs.* Long before they appear to belong as a "Christian" in our eyes they already belong to the Father as family. Why? Because God calls that which does not exist as though it already did. Each one is already part of the family in God's eyes; He is just hoping they start to recognize and believe it.

The father of the prodigal son didn't have to re-open his gates for his son's return because he still called him son the entire time he was away, and he kept his arms and gates wide open. Just because he was lost for a time never changed the fact that the father called him family; it only changed the son's willingness to be identified as family. The Father never lets go of the identity He gives us—it's just a matter of whether we will recognize, believe and come into this identity from our end. The Father never stops calling us son or daughter, whether we believe or not. Bottom line, we are His family, every single one of us, as well as everyone we encounter in mission or ministry. God is inclusive; however, just because He is inclusive doesn't mean He forces us to be His kids. He loves us so much that He lets us decide with our own free choice whether or not to enter into such belonging. Someone may choose not to believe, but that never means they don't belong. The Father sees every person through the eyes of belonging because, if not, how else will they ever believe? The Father's perspective is stronger than any ministry, prayer, process or program we can ever develop, and it's about time we start fully relying on His perspective to change the love, plans, actions and reactions that come out of us—even the ones that result from our best intentions.

But it's hard to believe in and love others that way if we ourselves do not yet know how the Father sees us. Do you realize how unconditionally you belong to God as one of the greatest treasures of His heart? Do you know how He sees you, the gleam in His eyes not just when you look at Him, but when He gets a glimpse of you? Do you know how He cherishes the unique makeup of your life? Do you know how excited He is to spend both eternity and *the now* with you? Can you fathom the reality that there is nothing you have to do to belong to Him? Nothing can change the fact that you belong to God! However, your belief does bring the necessary agreement from your side to accept such unconditional belonging and to enjoy house and family. But whether we yet grasp these truths or not, His hand is *always* stretched out, *always* calling you son or daughter, *always* calling you forward to be who you may have not yet realized you are. Our hand must be stretched out in a similar manner to everyone we encounter, starting with the beautiful perspective that each one already belongs to Him. We are not leading people to salvation as much as we are leading them to Him, their Father—revealing their belonging, making sure they know that Love Himself calls them son or daughter, even before *they themselves* believe. More than sharing with people our perspective about God, we through our lives and mission have the opportunity to reveal to people God's perspective of them, if we will value His perspective above our own. This truth is something I'm still very much learning, but it's a growing truth that I'm committed to living.

Moving Forward:

1. Describe the nature of the Father's perspective vs. ours in mission.

2. Why is the Father's perspective so important in mission? What powerful truth does His perspective communicate? How is it unconditional?

3. The Father's perspective is not based on what we do, but who we are in His eyes. Have you fully received the Father's perspective of unconditional love and belonging over your life?

Part 2: The Impact of God's Perspective

So it was, when they came, that he looked at Eliab and said, "Surely the LORD's anointed is before Him!" But the Lord said to Samuel, "Do not look at his appearance or at his physical stature, because I have refused him. For the Lord does not see as man sees; for man looks at the outward appearance, but the Lord looks at the heart." (1 Samuel 16:6-7)

I get razzed all the time for saying, "This is another favorite verse or passage" —but you know what? Sometimes it's just true! So I'm starting off this section with yet another favorite, likely with many more favorites to follow. So, sorry in advance—you'll have to forgive me.

But truly, I do love this verse. It's a truth that I try to find my life in, because I realize that how I see will dictate how I live. How I live greatly affects what flows out of my life towards others, and what flows out of my life towards others are the seeds that have a chance to multiply further than I can see—when I'm sowing from His perspective, that is.

Samuel was taught this vital truth from the Lord, and we can see why it was so important, because without Samuel operating by God's perspective, would we still have had God's chosen king in David? Obviously, God can still get things accomplished even if, and when, we mess this up. But He uses those who choose His perspective, who see the inward vision that He sees, to bring about His kingdom here on earth as it is in heaven. God is looking for those who will partner with Him in His perspective and therefore see abundant, even unlikely, harvests. Could Samuel have known the incredible fruit that would come from this one moment of choosing God's perspective over his own? David wasn't Samuel's first pick in this passage, God had to remind him. But Samuel was open to such a reminder, and the world was never the same because of it!

Each day when we encounter the one person or child in front of us, are you and I open to those reminders to see them as He sees them? Are we open to such an interruption even when we are already on a mission for God? What if Samuel had taken on God's original mission to go to Jesse's house and anoint a king, but had then gone about it by fulfilling it through his own eyes, or reason? Would the people have gotten Eliab as a king? Thankfully that didn't happen. That's why God did send Samuel, because God knew Samuel would be willing to be interrupted of his own perspective so that he could live and give according to God's. However, the birth of David's story goes back even further, to others who also saw with God's eyes.

The story of Boaz and Ruth is one that many of us have become familiar with. But it was their unique story that God used for me several years back to help re-define how He was calling us to do mission with Him—through His perspective.

In the world's terms, Ruth was a widow, very poor, and without income. Ruth faithfully chose to accompany Naomi to Bethlehem, a familiar area to Naomi, but burdening Ruth with yet another stigma of the time, that of a foreigner. They arrived in Bethlehem during the barley harvest, and the law at the time required all owners of harvest fields to allow the poor, widows, orphans and foreigners to glean from their fields. To "glean" essentially meant that those in need could take from the scraps, the edges, the corners and leftovers. When Ruth went out to glean on behalf of Naomi she found herself in a field owned by Boaz, a distant relative of Naomi's husband who had passed away. Ruth wasn't part of Boaz's family by blood, only by covenant. This is where the story started to bring about an unusual turn of events.

When Boaz saw Ruth enter his field, he had an opportunity of perspective thrust upon him. He could have just seen Ruth according to her need as one more person who was poor or hurting, entering his field to glean what she could as the law stated. But that's not what Boaz did! He inquired as to who Ruth was, and when he realized she was the daughter-in-law of Naomi, he immediately took on a new perspective—he now saw her as family, and this changed *everything!*

> *Then Boaz said to Ruth, "You will listen, my daughter, will you not? Do not go to glean in another field, nor go from here, but stay close by my young women. Let your eyes be on the field which they reap, and go after them. Have I not commanded the young men not to touch you? And when you are thirsty, go to the vessels and drink from what the young men have drawn." (Ruth 2:8-9)*

How many other field owners would have even taken the time or effort to see Ruth differently and go beyond their normal response or "ministry" to the poor? Boaz gave to her as if she was already a member of the house, showing her great favor. It both surprised and overwhelmed Ruth that Boaz would care for her in such an abundant manner, moving her heart and setting the stage for what God wanted to do in her life *beyond* meeting her immediate, physical needs—all because Boaz had altered his perspective.

> *So she fell on her face, bowed down to the ground, and said to him, "Why have I found favor in your eyes, that you should take notice of me, since I am a foreigner?" And Boaz answered and said to her, "It has been fully reported to me, all that you have done for your mother-in-law since the death of your husband, and how you have left your father and your mother and the land of your birth, and have come to a people whom you did not know before. The Lord repay your work, and a full reward be given you by the Lord God of Israel, under whose wings you have come for refuge." (Ruth 2:10-12)*

Boaz saw Ruth through God's eyes, seeing her as more than a project, seeing her heart, and recognizing that she really was family! By seeing Ruth through God's perspective, he was able to also respond to her through God's perspective. He did not simply "minister" to her—he showed her great love. He responded to her the way he would have responded to a close family member, as someone who already belonged. Boaz gave her protection, allowed her to drink freely and even invited her to come inside and dine with them at their table, again welcoming her as family. What is more, Boaz went to his laborers and instructed them to drop barley from their harvested bundles so that Ruth could glean not just from the leftovers or what could be spared, *but from the best parts.* I love that! Isn't that what the Father does for us? Ruth was privy to what was usually reserved for those already belonging to the house. Boaz lived towards her not by the law's perspective, nor even by his own. Boaz lived towards Ruth by the Father's perspective, and this grabbed Ruth's heart in an unusual way.

Ruth was so moved by the love and favor shown to her—as was Naomi upon hearing of what had taken place—that she went to Boaz and asked to be taken by him as his wife. We're told she handled herself properly and virtuously. Boaz didn't have to ask or try to convince Ruth to become part of the family; rather, it was she who longed to be part of a family in which she had already been shown such belonging.

Boaz stepped towards Ruth as his wife. Together, they had a child named Obed. Obed went on to have a child named Jesse. And Jesse—well, as we saw in the story of Samuel being sent by the Lord to Jesse's house, we know that Jesse had David, God's chosen king. Twenty-eight generations later, through this family line, Jesus Christ was born—Boaz and Ruth are part of the line of Christ! That is family according to God's perspective. *That* is multiplication.

Ruth, a foreigner, is included in the line of Christ. How is this possible? It all began with how Boaz saw Ruth. Boaz saw beyond her externals, beyond her needs and stigmas; he saw her according to God's perspective, which caused him to respond and love her differently—abundantly! Because Boaz loved her so abundantly she desired to be his wife and join the family. This allowed Boaz to approach her in an uncommon way, and from their lives, God brought forth uncommon fruit, a multiplication that became Christ Himself.

How often do we go out in mission or ministry and see people's needs, letting them glean from our lives what we can afford to give? All the while we are in pursuit of them, desperately seeking their salvation and hoping they'll cross that line and join us in God's family. But that's where Boaz differed—he wasn't trying to get Ruth to become part of the family; rather, he loved her from the Father's perspective as if *she already was* part of the family. It became therefore only natural for Ruth to desire such long-term belonging, having already tasted such unconditional, abundant love. Boaz stepped towards Ruth with God's perspective rather than his own, and incredible fruit came from their lives— God-sized fruit at that!

What might happen if we began to see and love others like this in mission? Instead of pursuing just the physical needs or the need for salvation in their lives, what if we simply began to love them abundantly according to the Father's perspective, as if they were family? Might they then *see* salvation rather than simply hearing about such a free gift? Don't you think they might get a taste of the true nature of the Father they've perhaps never known, and instead of running away, they might instead be the one running into His arms, running to take their place in the family and take up their purpose? What kind of fruit do you think this might birth through their lives? I can't predict the fruit, but I do know that it would be far more than I could ever bring about in their lives through ministry done from my perspective. Boaz modeled the Father's heart for Ruth, and everything changed from there. If we will see mission through the Father's eyes, we also will find ourselves living a renewed form of mission towards those He sees as family. The Father's perspective moves us from an agenda-based form of mission to a family-oriented, belonging-centered display of His abundant love. His perspective changes our response, and it changes how His children come to know their Father for themselves.

Moving Forward:

1. Imagine if Samuel hadn't stopped to listen and gain God's perspective before he acted. What is your "Eliab"? What "David" might God be pointing to instead?

2. How does seeing through the Father's eyes change our response in mission? Describe the power of showing belonging.

3. What might it look like for you to operate in mission the way Boaz did?

Part 3: The Father's Blessing

The Father's Blessing is one of the most underrated truths available to us in reaching out to and empowering others. I know this well, as it has had a profound personal impact on my life, and I have since watched God used it through my life to multiply far beyond my personal reach. The Father's Blessing is an impartation of sorts, a uniquely power-packed, public declaration of encouragement that helps to activate the unconditional love, value, approval and purpose that the Father has for us and to affirm God's belief in us.

Even Jesus received the Father's Blessing, clearly giving it value beyond just the old covenant traditions, establishing how vital God the Father deems it. He demonstrated its priority in giving it to His Son:

> *Then Jesus came from Galilee to John at the Jordan to be baptized by him. And John tried to prevent Him, saying, "I need to be baptized by You, and are You coming to me?"*
>
> *But Jesus answered and said to him, "Permit it to be so now, for thus it is fitting for us to fulfill all righteousness." Then he allowed Him.*
>
> *When He had been baptized, Jesus came up immediately from the water; and behold, the heavens were opened to Him, and He saw the Spirit of God descending like a dove and alighting upon Him.*
>
> *And suddenly a voice came from heaven, saying, "This is My beloved Son, in whom I am well pleased." (Matthew 3:13-17)*

Once again, we have a passage that is so familiar within Christian culture that we must take notice not to have it robbed of much of its power. The stage was set at Jesus' baptism, before Jesus' ministry, and the Father finds this moment so important that He opens the heavens, descends to earth like a dove over His Son and declares these unconditionally powerful words: *"This is My beloved Son, in whom I am well pleased."*

God wanted the world to know that this was His Son, whom He already valued and loved unconditionally, who carried tremendous purpose and whom He, the Father, approved of and believed in. That's one powerful affirmation! It is especially powerful when we remember that the Father gave this affirmation *before* Jesus had entered into His ministry, and *before* He had done any miracles or great works. This was not a conditional blessing. The Father found it so important to personally and publicly declare His approval over Jesus and His belonging to God that He made sure to show us that it wasn't because of anything Jesus had done or accomplished; rather, this blessing was given because of Who Jesus was, and is. The Father blessed His Son with what we often reserve for reward. If God Himself deemed this blessing necessary in order for Jesus to come into His purpose and calling as the Messiah, how much more important is it for us to release this same kind of unconditional, approving, empowering blessing over others in the world whom God already, in His sight, calls His own?

This Father's Blessing is what my dad and mom gave to me on my sixteenth birthday; it revolutionized my life beyond what I could know or describe in that moment, and I have never been the same because of it. My dad came to me just before my birthday and asked if I would be willing to let them to throw me a "blessing party" for my celebration that year. I was a little skeptical at first, dreaming of more grandiose sixteen-year-old ideas, but I could see that look in his eyes. So, reluctantly, I agreed. And with that, he asked me to take some time to prepare by reading Genesis 27:1-40 and the story of the blessing. Originally starting with Abraham, the blessing becomes uniquely relevant with Isaac, Jacob and Esau.

The night for my blessing party came, and many family friends gathered around and spoke out encouragements over me. Then, when it was my dad's turn, he and my mom stepped behind my chair, explained a little more, and then my dad began to read and pray over me a "Father's Blessing" that they had been preparing in prayer for a number of weeks. And much like the Father's blessing over Jesus, this blessing from my parents carried the Father's heart, blessing me with unconditional love and approval for *who* God made me to be, even and especially in the unique differences God purposed inside me. My dad communicated value to me for the person I was, and who I was becoming. He predicted great purpose still to come in God's plan and calling for my life. And as much as anything, in this blessing my dad demonstrated belief in me, and in the purpose God had for my life.

All around us every day people are striving, searching for worth, value and purpose. We all have an innate desire in us for this need to be met. All the while, God patiently loves us and waits for us to take our eyes off the many other sources from which we seek to glean worth, and instead learn to walk in the value, purpose and calling He already has for our lives. Too many people live their entire lives still striving in this search, never content, never realizing they have already been approved by the Father or that His approval is real even before they accomplish anything. As believers, we are as guilty of this as anyone. But this is where the Father's Blessing comes in—this is our opportunity to convey to one another, and to those who are lost, hurting or broken, just how valued they already are!

When I received that blessing from my dad and mom, my eyes, which had been searching horizontally every which way for what might bring me approval or worth, were suddenly set free— set free from the need to look for approval from man and free to look instead to God in order to receive and walk in the life, value and purpose God had for me all along. The Father's Blessing acts as a preface, a prelude, so that we release ourselves from the false things we are searching for and begin to realize whom *God* is searching for—us!

This Father's Blessing paved the way for the next few years of my life to be transformational in almost every way possible. A whole new world opened up as something in my heart and soul was met by that descending dove of God's Spirit, infusing peace into my search for meaning and setting a new course for me to live out my purpose *from* a place of meaning. The Father's Blessing answered my somewhat unconscious inner cry, and at the same time acted as a launching pad for living out God's unique best for my life, not measured by anyone else's. Not even one year later my dad passed away suddenly while on the mission field in Vietnam. I haven't had him physically by my side or in my corner now for sixteen years—yet, through that blessing, through that empowering impartation of unconditional love and approval that was straight from the Father Himself, modeled first towards His Son, my dad has been exceedingly present in my life ever since. I will never be the same, and now, because of how God has continued to multiply the Father's Blessing through my life, many others won't be either!

When my dad first asked me to read that original passage in Genesis 27:1-40 nothing stuck out right away. I simply read the passage and glossed over the familiar Bible story. But over the years as I have continued to realize what God did through that Father's Blessing, I have recognized parts of that passage as being overwhelmingly present in the world and in mission.

Usually, we look at Jacob in that passage and the incredible blessing he sought and received through Isaac. But do you know what, or who, sticks out to me? Esau does, for when I read his response after he traded away his birthright and watched it being given to Jacob, I feel like my heart can still literally hear his words. The Bible tells us that Esau, looking upon his lost blessing, let out a loud and bitter cry, "Bless me too, Father!" To me, that's where the Father's Blessing becomes such an opportune way of mission. Every single one of us has at some point in life, and perhaps very often, had that same loud cry in our heart, looking at man and the world the way Esau looked at Isaac, crying out to him; "Bless me, too!" All the while we know, with our minds at least, even if not always acknowledging it, that our Father in heaven hovers over each of us like He did His own Son, Jesus, waiting for us to look up and receive His Father's blessing of unconditional love, value and approval. When we impart this blessing to someone we release their eyes from looking to the world or man for purpose, and they are then freed to look up and see and live out what God was trying to show them all along.

Everywhere we go in life and everywhere we go in mission, we meet those like Esau, some quiet, some loud, but all with the same cry in their heart; just waiting for someone to listen closely enough to answer their cry. Many of us don't realize how much we have to give, if only to convey such an unconditional blessing to others and speak to their value and purpose. When we moved to Ethiopia and began to ask God how to join Him there, this became one of our primary strategies. We began spending a day each week at one particular orphanage in the countryside, home to eight children. We spent time with them, got to know them, watched and observed. All the while we prayed and took notes and asked the Father to show each of them to us from His perspective. With those notes from the Father, we prayerfully put together a Father's Blessing for each child in the orphanage and had each blessing translated, printed and framed with their picture.

The time came and we invited the eight children to spend the weekend with us at our home. We called it a "Pray & Play Weekend." I still look back at those three days together as one of the most memorable weekends of my life. We had very little furniture in our house. We had a refrigerator, a camp stove, one bed, a floor mattress for our daughter, one rug, a school table to gather around for meals and a stack of mattresses, blankets and pillows for the kids when they came. That was the full extent of our furniture, so it was a humble setting with the kids that weekend. Saturday night came amid our time together and we prepared a big meal—hamburgers and fries—and began to share with them the concept of this Father's Blessing. Then we invited the oldest boy to come forward to receive his blessing first. We gathered around him, read and prayed the blessing we had prepared and then invited all the other kids to join in speaking out encouragements and affirmations over his life. By the end of the time, I felt we had seen the sun rise over his life. The difference in his countenance was amazing, and from that point forward he rose up as a renewed leader of their sibling group of orphans. He helped us carry the Father's Blessing to every other child, exponentially increasing the involvement of each of the others. That night, the atmosphere was so thick with God's love and presence it felt like we experienced just a touch of what happened at Jesus' baptism—the Father breaking into the earthly scene, a passionate Father there to make sure His love and approval were known, *and felt*. We didn't have much to give the kids tangibly that weekend to meet or minister to their outer needs. What we did have was something the Father is longing to see imparted to every single one of His kids, a blessing on His behalf, releasing them from the life they are striving through so they might be free to take their eyes off the world and become locked in a gaze with Him—*Who is always looking upon them with unconditional love*. We can put so much emphasis on having physical resources to meet the external needs of others. And while this is necessary, there is this much deeper thing God is ready to do in and for each life, and it's something we already have free access to—His unconditional Father's heart.

The multiplication from the Father's blessing did not stop there. We continued to meet with the kids once a week to teach them how to draw near to God, spend time with Him and learn to go straight to the Source and hear His voice, and then every week we gave them each time to teach us what they were learning. Some of the things that came out of their hearts and mouths were astounding! We were blown away at what God was pouring into—*and through*—their lives. The next time we had them to our home for a "Pray & Play Weekend," we gave them a new assignment. We talked to them about the Father's Blessing once again and what it had meant to each of their lives. Then we talked about the many, countless kids in Ethiopia who live on the streets and might not even have the privilege of an orphanage as a home. We asked the kids, *"What do you think God wants to say to them? How might God want to share His Father's blessing with them as well?"*

We gave them pens and paper and sent them throughout the house to spend time with God and ask Him those questions. Then we asked them to write a letter to the kids on the streets, blessing them from the Father's perspective and using the answers they had come up with. Needless to say, we were humbled beyond words to read some of the letters and Father's Blessings that came back. Over the next few weeks we prayerfully compiled what the kids had written into one Father's Blessing, which we had translated and printed for the kids on the streets. From that point on, as we walked the streets and built relationships with new children, we would hold little gatherings in which to give them each their own Father's Blessing. I'll never forget one gathering, where we rented out the top floor of a restaurant and had so many of these kids from the streets walking up to us and asking for their pictures to be taken. And there they posed with bright smiles, blessings held up high, literally like they had just received their diploma, something usually acquired after a great, lengthy accomplishment. But these pieces of paper were different—pre-accomplishment—an extension of what the Father gave to His Son, and what my dad gave to me: unconditional love, value, approval and purpose, as well as an affirmation of his belief in me, even before we could do anything to earn it or prove our worth.

These same kids carried the spirit of this blessing to many others on the streets, often bringing them to our side and reminding us; "Hey, they need one, too!" Many kids came into God's family from all over the streets as a result of the Father's Blessing, all because eight "orphans," who had each received the Father's Blessing themselves, sought the Father's heart for others and simply wrote down what they saw in God's eyes for His kids. That is the power of the Father's Blessing. Whether it's Abraham giving it to Isaac, God giving it to Jesus, my dad imparting it to me, or eight children passing it on to their own peers on the streets—the Father's Blessing always multiplies!

Moving Forward:

1. Describe the nature of the Father's Blessing and why it carries such unseen power.

2. What is the "cry of Esau" and why is it important in mission?

3. How can you apply the Father's Blessing to your own life, your family and those around you, and those you will encounter in mission?

Part 4: Revealing the Father

"He who has seen Me has seen the Father." (John 14:9)

If there is one verse in my life I long to live out each day, it is this one. My prayer in any and every facet of life and mission is that this profound statement made by Jesus will be true in me. Anywhere I go, whomever I am with, I pray I will continue to be more and more transformed into the image of Him Who says, *"He who has seen Me has seen the Father."* That's what I want people to walk away saying. Not that I had a great ministry, spoke well, or any of that. I want others to walk away having felt like they encountered the Father through my life. That is my mission. That is essentially why I seek to be like Jesus in John 5:19 and join the Father where He is moving. I want to be so in sync with the Father's heart that it beats *through* me. In my eyes, that's the most effective form of mission I could live.

Oftentimes mission becomes result-focused, or, as we talked about previously, agenda-driven. However, results should be but the fruit naturally produced by our lives, fruit growing from our living connection with Him. If we will learn to love like Jesus, and focus on being Jesus to the world, then we will naturally become a walking revelation of the Father—just as Jesus always was.

St. Francis of Assisi once said, *"Preach the gospel always; when necessary use words."* It seems St. Francis really understood what Jesus meant when He said, *"He who has seen Me has seen the Father."* Of course, Jesus is the Son of God, so He bears the image of the Father. But then again, through the cross and His resurrection, so do we! Christ lives in us, right? Through Jesus, we have been made children of God, sons and daughters *of* our Heavenly Father, re-born in His image.

For as many as are led by the Spirit of God, these are the sons of God. For you did not receive the spirit of bondage again to fear, but you received the Spirit of adoption by whom we cry out, "Abba, Father." The Spirit Himself bears witness with our spirit that we are children of God. (Romans 8:14-16)

We carry our Father's image, each of us with a different part to live and reveal simply by being children of God, and it is His Spirit Who leads us in this mission. Mission is not so much about what we "do," it is first about who we are. Simply being a child of God who reveals the Father wherever you go is one of the greatest, most life-giving missions we can join Him in.

Now, this is where it can prove tempting to say something like, "This is how you reveal the Father—do it *this* way." But I'm going to try to avoid doing that because that's not how the Father sees our purpose and calling to reveal His kingdom and make disciples of all nations. That's not how the Spirit leads us, either. There isn't a cookie-cutter process for the best way to do mission, or a new trend you need to pick up; quite the contrary, actually. I believe that one of our number one goals in the mission of our lives should be—like Jesus—to reveal the Father wherever we go. But, *how* we do it—now *that* is a different and beautiful question that can only be answered between you and the Father.

My wife and I have five children, four girls and one boy. I know what you're probably thinking—our son really has himself surrounded, huh? But anyway, I, like most parents, am so grateful that my kids are so different in their personalities, their gifting, how they receive and show love, their physical traits, how they relate to my wife and me, and how they express their part of our family to the world around them. Their differences are part of what makes them so beautiful. Together, they make a more beautiful representation of who I am, or who my wife is, than any one of them could represent or reveal on their own. In fact, I'd be pretty sad and maybe even a little bothered if any of them tried to convince their siblings to do life, mission or whatever it may be in a manner that lined up more with their own ways. They each have a special, unique purpose they are called to live out to the world, and in doing so, although they might each reveal a part of my wife and me, I hope they will also reveal the Father.

In the "Father's Blessing" my dad gave to me, there is one line that has always stood out, one that I really believe reflects God's Father heart. However, it's not one I see us employ nearly enough, which is why I share it now. My dad said:

> *"I'm very proud to have you carry the LeTourneau name to future generations. I hope you don't believe that I think you're a lesser person because you're not like me in every area of life. That's a common belief among sons of type-A dads. The truth is that I think the best hope for the LeTourneau name lies in the very ways that you're different from me."*

I have come to find this to be a very profound and all-too-rare statement. Often, we are so bent on trying to conform others to our way of doing things that we can barely tolerate the differences in one another. Or we tolerate the differences just enough to avoid them while we focus on the other parts of people's lives, which we then refer to as their "strengths." But what if their differences—the differences we might not understand, or even sometimes judge— what if those are a big part of their strengths? What if we began to bless those differences in one another, as my dad spoke over me? Mission would become a lot more diverse and much further reaching. I cover this topic much more in depth in my book, *The Power of Uncommon Unity: Becoming the Answer to Jesus' Final Prayer*.[1] But the point is that often what is different in us will make a difference in the world. It is often this difference that we feel insecure about, and it's often this difference that is a specially created part of us that, when freely lived out, truly shines and reveals the Father through our lives—simply by our being who we are created to be.

This all sounds well and good, but in the world and culture in which we live—even in Christian culture—this is much easier said than done. But it is essential for us to learn if we are to live out our own unique mission in revealing the Father to the world. We can begin first by accepting our own differences and allowing ourselves the freedom to be different—not to conform but to freely shine! We often try to blend in and conform in an almost competitive way, secretly trying to "outdo" one another in the newest, most accepted or popular form of mission. But you have gifts that no one else has. You have a purpose that no one else can emulate. The Father has placed pieces of His heart in you that the world is desperately waiting for. So when you go out on a mission, or live mission in your daily life, you must know that the world is waiting not for your method of ministry or for your "results," but rather for a living revelation of the Father's unique image that He has placed within you.

The world needs to taste of the Father through your life. People have had plenty of the same dull, lifeless tastes over and over again—they are actually waiting for something different! They are waiting for you to allow the Father's true nature to be revealed through you. So, how do we reveal the Father in mission? It's simple. Be who God has made you to be, and live that out towards others. Don't try so hard to "do," but let Him naturally and freely overflow out of your life to anyone and everyone around you—whether on the mission field or in the grocery store. Your life reveals the Father much better than any agenda, program or format. Those are man-created; *you are God-created!*

Moving Forward:

1. How do you think the Father sees you?

2. What is a difference in your life, put there by your Heavenly Father, that you perhaps have tried to keep insecurely bottled up?

3. How might that special part of the Father's heart in you be lived out more freely, and how might it reveal Him to those you meet?

4. What does collaboration vs. competition look like to you in your area of mission?

End Notes:

1. Joey LeTourneau, *The Power of Uncommon Unity: Becoming the Answer to Jesus' Final Prayer* (Shippensburg, PA: Destiny Image Publishers, 2013).

CHAPTER 3:

THE SON IN MISSION

Even as I begin this chapter, I have sought out Jesus again just to ask Him what of His heart He wants us to know about His ways of mission, and how He wishes us to join Him. As I sought Him, I felt such a tender, yet powerful touch from His presence. I'm asking Him to lead us through this chapter the way He desires. And as much as anything, I'm asking you to request of Him the same. Still your heart, get away by yourself, ask Jesus how He sees mission and how He is calling you to join Him in His ways. But don't just ask—also take time to *listen!* Take those moments to be patient while still believing, and wait for Him to impress His presence upon you and make yourself vulnerable to what He is doing, how He is speaking, and how He wants to empower you in His ways going forward—even, and especially, if they require change and a deeper trust. Thank you for pressing in with Him, as this chapter will be worthwhile only to the extent that we make ourselves vulnerable to the work of His living presence and ways in our lives. And as we have already seen, when we allow Him to work freely in us and through us, the results are limitless!

Part 1: Revolutionary Jesus

Sometimes we see the word *revolution* and immediately place it in a box. It's a word we can file under the label of rebellion, or with other out-of-control or negative connotations. But through Jesus, revolution is a beautiful thing. Jesus was revolutionary—still is! *Revolutionary* is defined by dictionary.com as "radically new or innovative; outside or beyond established procedure." Um, I'm pretty sure Jesus took that definition to a whole new level, and I'm pretty sure that we are called to as well. As we have talked about already, it's easy to get into the already established flow of existing mission and its well-rounded existing definitions. But from the moment Jesus was conceived, His life was already re-defining life and mission in radically new and innovative ways, far beyond established procedure or comfortable process. I think it is safe to say that established procedure would not have had Jesus being conceived through a virgin, by the Holy Spirit. Are we so accustomed to that story now that we forget what the reality of it must have been like? What kind of stigmas do you think Joseph and Mary faced? We're not privy to all the details, but I'm sure— well, I know—that this method and claim of theirs was not considered common!

And speaking of which, measuring by what is deemed acceptable, I'm not quite sure Jesus' birth in a manger qualifies for how we would go about the mission of bringing God's Son into the world. *But that's the beauty of God's ways!* He operates differently than we do, and for a greater purpose. Our purpose is often to reach out, to help someone, to be recognized, to feel good, to do good, etc. God's purposes don't need our mission for self-filtering what He is pouring out. There are facets of self that have become culturally acceptable within ministry and mission that strip what is purely from Him and replace it with versions of outreach that validate us as much as they validate others. But living mission like Jesus usually costs us something on earth; whether that is security, reputation, success, worldly wealth or control. However, His ways of mission also sprout eternal fruit and build treasures and establish kingdom in ways that are impossible for us to reason or measure. When our mission is like that of Jesus, very little of what is accomplished actually happens on earth for our eyes to see. Far more is taking place in heaven! We join Him on earth in what can seem unique or revolutionary ways in our obedience in order for Him to accomplish much more in heaven. That's one of the greatest differences between Jesus' mission and what ours is usually built from. Jesus did mission from heaven's perspective. We often do mission from earth's, while keeping heaven in mind. But God wants to do so much more through each of our lives—a heavenly more—if we will trust Him with the earthly challenges along the way. Today, mission has a new "sex appeal" to it. That's not how it was for Jesus. That's not how it was for those like Hudson Taylor and others who had their coffins packed as suitcases when they departed for the mission field. I'm not saying we need to go to those extremes, but we do have to reconnect with what mission was like for Jesus if we are truly going to live Him out to the world.

Isaiah 61:1-2 is a great example. It's the passage Jesus spoke when announcing His mission in the synagogue at the beginning of His ministry in Luke 4.

> *"The Spirit of the Lord is upon Me, because He has anointed Me to preach the gospel to the poor; He has sent me to heal the brokenhearted, to proclaim liberty to the captives and recovery of sight to the blind, to set at liberty those who are oppressed; to proclaim the acceptable year of the Lord." (Luke 4:18-19)*

For us, this has become a popular passage and statement. We understand it now. But when Jesus announced it, it was anything but popular. That's not how you did mission back then, or the types of people to whom you reached out. There was not the flare of grandiose one-liners or great Christian headlines. There was no earthly self-worth to be gained, in fact, quite the contrary. When Jesus finished speaking about this passage the people wanted to throw Him over a cliff. But He trusted God. He kept His eyes on the Father. He kept joining Him one step at a time, obedience over self-initiated mission. Obedience to the fresh, living word of God is true mission. That is what Jesus modeled. He was revolutionary because He stayed on the path of heaven even while upon earth. His mission had as many "haters" as anyone, and they didn't even have the Internet yet to broadcast Him as a heretic. They had a cross for that. But the cross was only one more step on His revolutionary path of mission—a path of revolutionary love that would change the world. Why? Because Jesus was free to be different. He was free to please the Father above man. He was free on the inside in a revolutionary way—a freedom all too scarce today. Jesus was a revolutionary in His words, His deeds, His perspective, His love and in His blood. Man won't give us the freedom to do mission this way; such freedom only comes from the Father as we do everything out of union with Him.

I've grown up as a people pleaser, no doubt. But that's also probably why God started to lead my family and me—one step at time—by obedience to His voice on a path that has turned out to be quite revolutionary. See, I still want to please people, it's just that I want to please Him *even more*. I want to stay in alignment with God more than with man, or mission. That's what Jesus did, and as a result, mission was revolutionized. Isaiah 61 and Luke 4 are common for us now, but only because He walked those dry paths and worked that unplowed ground when it was anything but obvious to the world or religious culture around Him.

The same should be true for us. We're not to try to be radical for the sake of being radical, and I am not saying to throw caution to the wind or abandon wisdom. But I am saying we're not to live by fear—or fear of man—and disguise it as wisdom. We are called to live and love like Jesus, and I can't imagine that our pre-conceived plans of ministry often fall in line with His revolutionary ways.

Again, revolutionary isn't something we must try to be, but it is something we must be willing to be. We are often afraid of "revolutionary" because it leaves us out of control, but the question I then have to ask myself is: *"Do I really want to be in control? Am I supposed to be in control? Or am I willing to let Him lead and show me His unseen ways? Why do we think we need to stay in control in mission? Can we not trust Him more than we can trust ourselves?"*

We now have hindsight to look back on Jesus' ways with greater understanding, but how would we have counseled Him if we had been there? I think we might have used our good sense to caution and protect Him from going outside the lines. Can you imagine our good intentions? *"Lord, what will people think if you associate with her?" "Teacher, you can't say that here, we have to be careful!" "Jesus, remember, today is the Sabbath, we still need to be honoring." "Master, you musn't give yourself up to death!"* Just read through the New Testament and I'm sure you will see a ton of additional examples that, in the moment, we would have warned against, too. But thankfully, Jesus always did what He saw His unseen Father doing—even if it could be called ill-advised or different. He truly walked by faith and not by sight. Now *that* is revolutionary. I can't imagine where we'd be if Jesus wasn't revolutionary. Would we know His love like we do? Would we understand the ways God's kingdom works through His eyes and not just our own? Would we have a love so vital and real that it spreads through us, person to person? Would a cross of crucifixion be a symbol of love and redemption that we wear around our necks? Revolutionary isn't just a dynamic description to use or teach; it is a necessity, an essential for the kingdom to be established on earth as it is in heaven. We can't know the Son in mission without surrendering ourselves to His revolutionary ways.

There is one particular scene in the movie *Amazing Grace* that I can't help but laugh at and be drawn to. William Wilberforce is one of my absolute heroes, and when he was in the middle of fighting for the abolition of the slave trade, he too was considered a revolutionary—and that was not meant as a compliment. Typically, revolutionaries and their noble battles aren't respected or seen in a positive light during *their* time. It's not until years later that we usually recognize that they were right all along, and we come to know their early ways or teachings as familiar. But Wilberforce shook off the labels thrown at him and kept moving forward in the unique mission God led Him in for that time. In one scene in the movie, which shows a lively debate between Wilberforce and other leaders of the House of Commons, the opposing leader stands and declares about Wilberforce and his mission: *"Revolution is like the pox, it spreads from person to person."*[1]

Now, this opposing leader obviously meant this in a negative fashion, comparing revolution to a terribly contagious disease such as the pox. But to me, this only highlights his fear of what is possible. When we fear something, or someone, we try to quarantine it, like the pox. We want to stay in control and keep it from spreading. That's why we become so afraid of revolution, because it takes a change we might not yet be comfortable with and spreads it faster than we can control. But that's also the beauty of being revolutionary in mission; the kingdom can spread in its most raw, pure form from person to person. We don't have to be in control as long as we are surrendered to His. We must let Him take our mission outside our well-meaning lines and spread His love in His revolutionary way, more virally than we can ever divvy out on our own.

Moving Forward:

1. How many aspects of Jesus' life and mission, from birth through resurrection, can you name that were revolutionary for His time, or any time for that matter?

2. You may know Isaiah 61/Luke 4 as a familiar or popular verse now. But discuss why it would have been a

revolutionary form of mission in that time. Talk about the fear of man and why it keeps us from being revolutionary like Jesus.

3. Being revolutionary in mission is not being rebellious in mission. Talk about the difference. How can you be revolutionary while still carrying out love and honor?

Part 2: Receiving in Mission

Initially, receiving in mission may come across like somewhat of an oxymoron. I mean, isn't receiving supposed to be the opposite of *doing* mission? Isn't *receiving* somewhat selfish in nature in the face of those in need? I thought mission wasn't supposed to be about us. And it isn't! However, that is exactly the reason why receiving is so vital within the context of mission—a counter-cultural form of mission goes much further than need-deep. Receiving is often a counter-intuitive way to put another person before yourself, an opportunity to let go of seeking your own worth through giving, and allow the other person to gain worth by your receiving what they can give to you. And there you run into the most basic and natural rule for why receiving is essential—because you cannot really give until you have first taken time or had the opportunity to receive. Jesus demonstrated each of these components of receiving in His life and mission, and so must we.

His Baptism: *"Then Jesus came from Galilee to John at the Jordan to be baptized by him. And John tried to prevent Him, saying, 'I need to be baptized by You, and are You coming to me?' But Jesus answered and said to him, 'Permit it to be so now, for thus it is fitting for us to fulfill all righteousness.' Then he allowed Him." (Matthew 3:13-15)*

John didn't even have to ask Jesus, quite the contrary actually. Jesus went to John asking to receive, knowing how needed this was. Jesus easily could have reasoned that it was unnecessary; I mean, He is the Son of God and all, so it would have been pretty understandable to simply say, "Nah, I'm good. I'm above that." That is after all how John was reasoning as he spoke with Jesus. But Jesus saw the situation differently; He saw Himself differently. Jesus knew that receiving something such as a baptism wasn't beneath His mission, but would actually help fulfill it to the greatest possible extent. Jesus' mission didn't only embrace receiving—it began that way.

Alone with the Father: *"However, the report went around concerning Him all the more; and great multitudes came together to hear, and to be healed by Him of their infirmities. So He Himself often withdrew into the wilderness and prayed."* *(Luke 5:15-16)*

I love that phrase: *"So He Himself often withdrew into the wilderness and prayed."* There is so much to be found in it. You can almost break it down one word at a time and find immense power in each word. I won't go that far for the sake of space, but let's look a little deeper at what this meant for Jesus, and what it means in mission for us now. The passage shows us that Jesus' calling and mission were really taking off. Multitudes were gathering and there were many, many needs that must have been adding up. But we can see that though He was need able, He was not need driven. He knew the priority of being filled up in times away, alone with the Father, so that He would have something of true worth to give when the time was right. Nothing has changed my life and mission more than my times alone with God, learning to receive directly from Him.

Also, notice how it says, *"He Himself often withdrew into the wilderness."* Usually, our wilderness seasons have to almost hit us over the head before we realize our need to embrace that time of oneness with Lord and receive from Him. But Jesus was proactive in His desperation, putting Himself in position to receive and be filled before becoming depleted. Jesus knew that receiving from the Father was vital to giving life to others in mission with the Father. He didn't wait for the wilderness to come to Him; He purposefully went there proactively.

And last, not only was Jesus proactive in such receiving, He also went away like this *often.* Jesus didn't take receiving from the Father lightly. He didn't make it a quick devotion to cross off the list. This time alone with the Father was central to His ability to join the Father in His ways of mission. Jesus often went away to receive because He knew that ability to give happens in direct proportion to time taken to receive. Jesus' own mission was fueled by these frequent, proactive times away from where the needs threatened to dictate the agenda. He did not sustain His worth by meeting the needs, but rather by being filled by the Father so that others could find greater worth as well.

Anointing at Bethany: *"Then Mary took a pound of very costly oil of spikenard, anointed the feet of Jesus, and wiped His feet with her hair. And the house was filled with the fragrance of the oil. But one of His disciples, Judas Iscariot, Simon's son, who would betray Him, said, 'Why was this fragrant oil not sold for three hundred denarii and given to the poor?' . . . But Jesus said, 'Let her alone; she has kept this for the day of My burial. For the poor you have with you always, but Me you do not have always.'"* *(John 12:3-8)*

Few passages in scripture mean more to me than this one, for a variety of reasons. What stands out to me in regard to our topic is the difference of priority in mission between Mary and Judas, and most notably, which one Jesus agreed with. Mary came to Jesus with her value, not just in offering the perfume but also in how she let down her hair to wash His feet—which was a very vulnerable, pride demolishing act on her part—and gave her mission to Jesus. Judas meanwhile, despite not having true intentions for the poor, argued for a more practical kind of mission, trying to shame Mary for not having the right priorities.

I think we can all feel this battle inside us sometimes. We feel the Holy Spirit moving our heart in a unique direction with Him, but we hear that more religious, reasoned voice as well, trying to shame us into a more outwardly sacrificial form of mission, albeit perhaps a great one when carried out with the right motives, at the right time. This may be the very reason we find "receiving" to be a difficult form of mission to embrace personally. It is easy to reason ourselves away from some of Jesus' personal priorities, which is why we mustn't ever let go of the pursuit to stay fresh with Him, constantly seeking His perspective in each circumstance so as to always maximize His love and all He's made available to us.

Look how Jesus responds. He didn't take the religious side or viewpoint of what expected mission should look like—the very kind we often assume to be the only way, fearing we're otherwise being irresponsible like Judas said of Mary. Instead, Jesus knew the value of what it meant in that special moment for Him to receive something that would leave a fragrant offering on His mission forever. Jesus knew that He, even as the Son of God, needed to receive, and He recognized the power in allowing Mary to give. That concept to me is just crazy and overwhelming.

You might be on a mission trip where the Lord is excited because in His eyes, He finally has you away from busyness and all to Himself. And though you're tempted to engage, there might be guilt to go out and *do* more or *give* more instead of quiet yourself with Him. And that doing and giving will come. But you know what? Jesus, through the passages above, gives you permission to pull back from doing and giving when you feel Him beckoning. He wants you to Himself, where you can receive from Him, but also where He can receive from you. Don't reserve your entire offering—whether time, treasure or talents—for the poor; and that's coming from someone who loves to give. Bring your offering to Jesus first and He will direct you to others from there. He wants to receive from you, and He will multiply through you in mission for the sake of the poor as well. He has a much bigger picture in mind than the needs we can see. Jesus knew and lived the power of receiving in mission because He knew that receiving is not a selfish form of mission—no matter how many religious voices may shame you into thinking that—receiving is a further-reaching one.

This power of receiving came alive for us personally while working with kids from the streets in Ethiopia. We truly relied on our times in God's presence each day before we would go out in mission, and we couldn't have gone forward like we did without those times. But most of all, our minds were blown as we found out what meant the most to those we were ministering to, as it wasn't always what we could give them or what we expected; nor was it always even related to their very apparent, external needs.

We were very purposeful as we began our time in the country to find ways to receive. The last thing we wanted to do was to make those we were reaching out to further dependent on us and what we could offer them, whether physically or spiritually. The people needed to be empowered, which meant that often we needed to step back and let them lead.

Sometimes this happened in a small way and sometimes as a bigger form of empowerment, and other instances were very unique in nature. For example, we didn't have a vehicle for our family during our entire three years in Ethiopia. We wanted one but quickly saw the value God was creating by our lack of a car. It caused us to use taxis, with many of the drivers becoming close family friends, and with some of whom we actually spent holidays. It also kept us walking the streets, meeting people, connecting through smiles and forging unlikely relationships in hidden but fertile grounds.

The lack of a vehicle also married well with our strategy in learning the language. We prayed about it when we moved to Addis Ababa and really felt we weren't supposed to go to language school; instead, we were to ask the locals wherever we went to be our teachers, further allowing them in on the journey. This created so many good laughs and enjoyable, lasting connections. We learned the language from so many different people: Staff members and residents taught us when we visited an orphanage, the street kids found so much joy in teaching us on their turf, taxi drivers were very demanding and specific in making sure we learned correctly as we rode with them, and during our daily visits to the various shops around our area, shopkeepers and customers kept us challenged and learning with great camaraderie among neighbors. Basically, without a car or a language class we were vulnerable, which allowed the locals to rise up with added purpose in our lives.

Now, it wasn't a one-way relationship of dependence; rather, it was a joint walk forward into new territory, and an incredible journey at that! This relationship was also very effective with the kids we were working with. Instead of simply teaching them, we gave them what we called "God Journals" that they used as they took time to inquire of the Lord each day, learning to hear His voice and to depend on Him as their Source. Then, when we gathered back together, the kids taught us. They were so excited every week to go through their pages and share what God was teaching them, what He was speaking to their hearts about, and how it impacted all our lives. We gained so much just by listening, and this opportunity to lead us, as well as one another, helped them step forward far beyond anything else we could have offered them.

But perhaps my favorite realization of receiving in mission came during our frequent lunch gatherings with the kids from the streets. As you can imagine, many of the kids were quite hungry. Many had missed several meals before we'd meet them at a restaurant for a big feast. The kids would funnel in one or two at a time, sometimes in groups, and always making their entrance known. They were ready to eat, but more than just the food, they were excited to see us, and one another. For those of you who aren't familiar with it, Ethiopian food is very unique. You eat with your hands using torn pieces of *injera;* a spongy, rolled type of bread that is utilized to pick up combinations of meats, veggies and sauces. They have a tradition in their culture built around food and mealtimes together called *gousha*. This is when someone at the table picks up a few fingers full of food within a bit of injera, and they reach across to feed you by hand. We were caught off guard the first time someone reached across the table to feed us, but we quickly learned how special to them this tradition is.

The kids from the streets loved showing us this tradition more than just about anything! Of course we'd have them each wash their hands when coming into the restaurant before eating (for their own sake as much as ours), but still, you can imagine the thoughts and decisions going through our minds looking across and seeing these precious little hands that at any given time could be grimy with snot or even cuts and dirt. In that moment, we had a decision to make; we could shake the children off and focus on the food that their hungry little bellies should be eating, or we could let them reach their mysteriously covered little hands into our mouths and feed us. While still engaging wisdom, we learned quickly that saying yes to letting them feed us was one of the most powerful things we could do. It brought them so much joy!

Here you have children who are living on the streets, rarely eating even close to enough, joining you for a feast at a restaurant they would almost never venture into. And yet, it's not the food that we could feed them that meant the most to them, but the food that we allowed them to feed us. How's that for counter-cultural? It's still confounding for me to think about. Their stomachs may have desperately needed the food, but even more so their hearts desperately needed to be given value and worth, which they received as we allowed them to be "givers" in our lives.

This is completely the opposite of how we often view our role in mission or ministry. We are driven to give, but can easily miss out on the moments that might just give even more—through receiving. Those bites of food and moments together during gousha brought more sustained worth and connection than anything we could have given or taught. We had to realize that we were seeing the original intent of our mission towards them only in part, and we had to allow them to give us the other part of mission that too often goes missing. External needs, as well as our need to be needed, will always be demanding in almost any form of mission we enter into. But we must not allow these demands of the world to override the needs of hearts that can be fulfilled through our receiving.

Moving Forward:

1. Why does receiving in mission appear to be an oxymoron?

2. Looking at Jesus' personal priority on receiving in mission, what aspect stands out most to you? How can you apply it to your life?

3. Talk about why the street kids in Ethiopia might have been more blessed by feeding us than by us feeding them. How did that give them value?

Part 3: Moved with Compassion

Compassion, as well as our interpretation of it, can easily lead us into the great deep of the misunderstood. It's bigger and deeper than we usually realize, and more powerful than the emotions we often ascribe to it. Compassion was among the most powerful things at work through the heart of Jesus and was often found to be a transformative power behind His life and mission. Jesus didn't just have or possess compassion in mission; He was fueled by compassion towards greater mission. Compassion is not just a small-scale reaction in the moment but also a big-picture purpose of redemption. We often regard it solely as an emotional form of outreach, but it is also a catalyst for strategic discipleship.

Then Jesus went about all the cities and villages, teaching in their synagogues, preaching the gospel of the kingdom, and healing every sickness and every disease among the people.

But when He saw the multitudes, He was moved with compassion for them, because they were weary and scattered, like sheep having no shepherd.

Then He said to His disciples, "The harvest truly is plentiful, but the laborers are few. Therefore pray the Lord of the harvest to send out laborers into His harvest." (Matthew 9:35-38)

This passage grabs me in that there are three layers present and all are necessary to the way we learn about and live out the compassion of Jesus in mission. At first, Jesus was *moved in the moment.* *"Then Jesus went about all the cities and villages, teaching in their synagogues, preaching the gospel of the*

kingdom, and healing every sickness and every disease among the people." In this way, He went about His mission meeting the needs of the people and operating in what we often view as the lone component of compassion: See a need, feel the need, meet the need. This was actually a very powerful part of Jesus' mission; the only problem for us comes when we make it the *only* way we live out our compassion. If you look throughout the gospels, so many of Jesus' miracles were preceded by a statement similar to, *"He was moved with compassion."* This happened before the feeding of the five thousand, before the feeding of the four thousand, and more. But still, we must remember that Jesus' compassion was love based—He was moved to action from a motive of purposeful love. We often think of these momentary acts of compassion and relate it to sympathy, emotion or even guilt. But Jesus' moments of outstretched compassion to love on and meet the needs of the people were all love driven; He saw from the Father's heart and was compelled to release this love into the person before Him, thereby revealing the kingdom and the gospel.

Emotion-based and love-based compassion in mission can feel very similar. But one is a reaction of self, with all the different motives and emotions we have inside of us mixing with our kingdom intentions. The other is pure and straight from the heart of God—an invitation to join Him in touching someone's life. From this place, there is no striving out of self, but instead we are literally being moved to action in the moment because the heart of God is ready to beat through us, beyond our capabilities and gifting, releasing a form of love so heavenly that we can neither conceive nor limit it on our own. Why else do we read in this passage that Jesus healed *every* disease and *all* who were sick? It's because He moved out of such pure love *with* the Father. When we are so engaged with the Father first, like Jesus was, well-intentioned reactions of self are replaced with unstoppable love. This sort of compassion is less about what we do, and more about where, or Whom, we operate from.

Second, there was a *realization of greater purpose*. The first layer showed the smaller-scale version of compassion moving through Jesus in the moment. This second layer is where Jesus begins to address a bigger root issue than what is externally obvious. In acknowledging this second layer, He determines a big part of His own purpose going forward. *"**But when He saw the multitudes, He was moved with compassion for them, because they were weary and scattered, like sheep having no shepherd.**"* Whereas Jesus first demonstrated the power of compassion in need-oriented works, I love the sudden transition of vision towards the bigger issue at hand—a transition He also calls us towards. Jesus saw that not only were there external needs present and waiting to be met, His compassion saw a greater movement waiting to be joined, one that plucked at His heart's purpose and drove Him beyond the moment, lifting others beyond the moment as well. This is part of the compassion transition the Lord is calling us to in mission, a step beyond where we often leave compassion to reside, a unique purpose in each of our hearts waiting for our answer.

Jesus' compassion showed Him the cultural need present in that time that awaited the very identity and purpose He naturally carried. The very same can be true for us if we'll embrace compassion in our hearts in this larger way, and realize that a mission even greater than the moment is waiting to be birthed. Jesus wasn't looking only at the sickness and disease, but also at the internal issues that caused the people to be as weary and scattered as sheep. By expressing compassion for the unguided sheep, He began to declare His calling as our true Shepherd, a pro-active purpose designed to address the root of the issues before His eyes.

The same can be said for us as we allow the Lord to lead us into this deeper layer of compassion in mission. It is natural to see and be compelled by various needs. And you will be called to meet some of them. But there comes a moment when our compassion grabs all the pieces of our heart that have broken for those around us and begins to join God in putting the puzzle back together—a bigger picture than one piece can reveal—demonstrating the purpose all those pieces have come together to create, and leading us towards the field in which we may be called to sow or reap long term. What is the bigger purpose God is calling you to within mission? Compassion with the Father is often your first indicator and identifier. Compassion leads us to what we are passionate about at a heart level. And our passions lead us to the purpose the Father has been waiting for us to join Him in. Compassion begins in the moment, but it also acts as a guide towards our long-term purpose.

The third layer of compassion in mission that Jesus reveals to us in this passage is seeing compassion as a catalyst for discipleship. Look where Jesus transitions to next: *"Then He said to His disciples, 'The harvest truly is plentiful, but the laborers are few. Therefore pray the Lord of the harvest to send out laborers into His harvest.'"* After we recognize our greater purpose, we must see the possibilities at hand for joining the Lord in empowering multiplication. When compassion shows us our bigger purpose, suddenly our eyes are opened to see the vast, ripe, plentiful fields just waiting to be harvested. Compassion now looks beyond just the needs of the moment, beyond even the individual long-term purpose, and sees the unique opportunity calling for others to step into their special role.

Now, we see those we may have simply felt sorry for before as those who might also be leaders in their own way, as those God is calling you to empower in their own purpose and calling. Compassion has progressed from meeting their external need, to recognizing and addressing the internal root cause, and finally to empowering them for their own mission, resulting in exponential multiplication through their lives.

God led us through this progression with the street kids in Ethiopia. The vision He gave us was not simply to help them survive, but to help them thrive and flourish in their own mission. We wouldn't be the ones going out to the other kids on the streets, they would! The kids had a great authority because of what they had overcome, and now our compassion was directed towards motivating *their* action, rather than just our own. That is what Jesus was showing us in the third layer of that passage. Jesus revealed to the disciples the vision that birthed His compassion. No longer was just one person being moved to act in the moment; now it was a movement of multiplication. Compassion has a multi-faceted power about it that progresses from the moment, to long-term purpose, to enduring multiplication. All three are good in themselves, but in order to have far-reaching, God-birthed effect, all three must learn to be embraced in mission together.

Too often we reserve compassion in mission as something bound only to evangelism and outreach, but it has greater purposes in store. Jesus did not limit it to the first in-the-moment layer, which resulted in the fruit that saw every sickness and disease healed or need met, as good as these things were. How often do we stop here and start to gather fruit? Jesus saw differently. He looked beyond that fruit to join God and go even further. Compassion sees beyond that momentary layer to which we often relegate it and beckons us to open our eyes not only to the one in front of us now, but also to the One who is leading us both into larger places.

Moving Forward:

1. What does it mean to you for your heart to be moved by compassion towards the one in front of you? How did Jesus walk in this way?

2. How might you transition from meeting immediate, external needs to letting your heart be moved with compassion towards the deeper-rooted purposes to which God might be wanting to direct you? How might compassion reveal your passion and help identify your purpose?

3. Think about and brainstorm ways you might be able to not only meet someone's external needs, but begin to take compassion further and disciple them to help meet those same needs for others in their culture.

Part 4: Love Them, Love Them, Love Them!

We arrived to live in Ethiopia early in 2008 with a surplus of possibilities, a lot of transition to work through and a whisper in our hearts saying, *"I have a better way, just ask."* My wife, Destiny, was pregnant, and our only daughter at that time was five years old. Our funds were low and we were living a day at a time in a guesthouse until we had provision for basic appliances and furniture to move into the home we were renting. We had few certainties at the moment other than the fact that Jesus was calling us forward on an adventure with Him—*one step at a time.* We didn't have the answers, but He did. So, we trusted Him and began to move forward, filling our days by asking lots of questions of people, walking the streets asking Jesus for His vision and perspective, and lying on our faces inquiring of the Lord as to what He was doing and how we were to join Him. It wasn't long until He was blowing all our plans out of the water and unveiling an unexpected but unforgettable path.

The more we inquired of God for His ways and purposes the more He kept taking us back to one particular passage as our starting point—Isaiah 58. The passage—in my Bible at least—is labeled *"Fasting That Pleases God."* If you're familiar with Ethiopia you may know that fasting is very prevalent in their culture. However, this is a different kind of fast. It's not a fast from food or anything else we usually expect; to me, *it's a fast of love, a fast from self.*

"Is this not the fast that I have chosen: To loose the bonds of wickedness, to undo the heavy burdens, to let the oppressed go free, and that you break every yoke? Is it not to share your bread with the hungry, and that you bring to your house the poor who are cast out; when you see the naked, that you cover him, and not hide yourself from

your own flesh?

"Then your light shall break forth like the morning, your healing shall spring forth speedily, and your righteousness shall go before you; the glory of the Lord shall be your rear guard. Then you shall call, and the Lord will answer; you shall cry, and He will say, 'Here I am.'

"If you take away the yoke from your midst, the pointing of the finger, and speaking wickedness, if you extend your soul to the hungry and satisfy the afflicted soul, then your light shall dawn in the darkness, and your darkness shall be as the noonday. The Lord will guide you continually, and satisfy your soul in drought, and strengthen your bones; You shall be like a watered garden, and like a spring of water, whose waters do not fail. Those from among you shall build the old waste places; you shall raise up the foundations of many generations; and you shall be called the Repairer of the Breach, The Restorer of Streets to Dwell In.

"If you turn away your foot from the Sabbath, from doing your pleasure on My holy day, and call the Sabbath a delight, the holy day of the Lord honorable, and shall honor Him, not doing your own ways, nor finding your own pleasure, nor speaking your own words, then you shall delight yourself in the Lord; and I will cause you to ride on the high hills of the earth, and feed you with the heritage of Jacob your father. The mouth of the Lord has spoken." (Isaiah 58:6-14)

To tell you the truth, even recounting this passage now grabs my heart back to those moments as if I'm right there once again. We prayed and spoke out this passage every day and it quickly became more than a passage—it became a map of the steps Jesus was leading us to walk with Him. If you notice, these verses read like a living map of what Jesus' life and mission looked like all across the gospels. We felt like He was calling us to join Him in the same. So, we went on a different sort of fast. Though we had a role in a wonderful, worldwide organization at the time and there was much to do to get started, we felt like we were supposed to fast from any organized ministry or programs, and from all *our* agendas for our first forty days in country. During those forty days our agenda would be this: Walk the streets with Jesus according to Isaiah 58 and ask Him to teach us to see as He sees, to walk as He walked and to love as He loves.

Our ministry and mission was turned upside down one day and one step at a time. Still, we couldn't have been more thrilled! God began doing things on the streets that we never could have planned or created on our own. He started connecting us to children and families who lived on the streets as well as former street kids who were now young adults with hearts primed to be empowered into their own harvest field. One person at a time, the Father started using these daily walks across the city of Addis Ababa—and I mean the whole city—to see His family built amid broken, unlikely surroundings.

I'll never forget the first two children we met in a rough part of town, an area that became like our second home for a while. We were walking past a mosque one day—Destiny five months pregnant and our daughter Mercy by our side—all of us blonde-haired, blue-eyed and standing out like a very sore thumb. Two girls came dashing across the street to grab our hands. I can still see their faces today like they were our own kids. But they were the Father's own! Neither girl asked for a thing, which was a very rare instance considering we were foreigners. Instead, they just held our hands and walked with us for many blocks until we were approaching a compound where we had a meeting. They spoke little English, and we were still very new to learning Amharic. All of a sudden they stopped, faced us and said, *"We're Muslim, you're Protestant,"* with a quizzical look on their faces. "Yeah," we said, "So what?" We shrugged our shoulders and then they did, too. We bought some snacks for them before we left, and that was our day. However, our hearts were on fire because of what we felt in these two precious girls.

The next day we were walking the same path, and now it wasn't just these two girls, but six others of their friends suddenly came with them, bounding across the street. This time, they *all* jumped on us. And once again, we walked together for a good ten blocks, thoroughly enjoying one another's company even with few words to share the entire way. The next day, walking the same path, these two girls and eleven more of their friends came flying across the streets to maul us, then walked with us across the city yet again. These were some of the most life-changing steps of our lives. We were supposedly "fasting" from organized mission and ministry, but God was growing something far greater, a form of mission that was near to His heart, simply through our seeking to walk in the steps of Jesus and how He lived mission. We had designs on setting up a big youth prayer and empowerment center. We wanted to build God a house. But instead, God was making *us* into a house. We wanted, like David, to build God a physical structure where people could experience His presence (2 Samuel 7:1-5). But God, as He did with David, wanted to make our lives into a family-structure kind of house, built through multiplication and a growing family line—spiritually speaking, at least (2 Samuel 7:11). God was establishing His family structure all across the streets. God was building something our eyes couldn't see, fruit that we couldn't gather or call our own. It was an unseen house whose foundations were in the hearts of His people, rather than in any building or ministry. And yet, it all began so simply. We fasted from our ways of ministry, and Jesus showed us His steps instead—what a beautiful trade!

This form of mission with the Lord was punctuated one late night during a time with the Lord. The electricity had been out for fourteen or fifteen hours that day, and the rest of the family was headed to bed. I was sitting in the dark at our dining room table with my computer on its last five percent of battery. I wanted to log back on to finish a couple more things but felt a strong nudge on my heart from the Lord. *"Not now,"* He said. *"I have something for you; come to Me instead."*

I closed my computer and sat staring forward into the dark, silent, trying to still myself before the Lord and give Him room to lead me. Before I go any further I want to explain something to you—I'm not a sensationalist by any means. I don't like to exaggerate anything; in fact, I'll usually tone it down because I'd rather be true and accurate than grandiose. We have had some pretty miraculous stories watching God move, meet us or speak to our hearts, but they are more simple, or normal, than we often think. I've come from a wide background of church experiences and beliefs, and I treasure them all. So please understand, as I share this "vision" or "experience" with you, that my focus is not on the experience itself as much as on the very tangible way God brought His word and love to life.

Anyway, I had closed my computer and was waiting on the Lord there in the dark. It was quiet and peaceful. Suddenly, I was in a vision with Jesus at my side, inviting me up from my seat. He put His arm around my shoulder and began to walk me slowly around the living room. *"Do you want to walk the streets as I walked them?"* He asked. *"Of course! Please!"* I answered readily. *"I'll show you."*

It wasn't some long journey; rather, in total it consisted of only fifteen feet or so between our dining room and family area. After the first few steps He stopped me and said, *"First, you must see as I see."* As He said these words I saw an image of an old, tattered woman crouched before us. Her outward appearance was dark and dirty, and she was draped in torn fabric. But there was a bright sort of light that appeared to be trying to escape from every crevice of her body. She looked like what happens when you go into a dark room and put a flashlight under your enclosed fist; the dark of your outer flesh covers the light, but you can see a glow of the light trying to escape from every crack or crevice possible, distinguishing the difference between the flesh of your hand and the light inside. This is exactly how she appeared. Her outer, fleshly appearance tried to hide the light, but Jesus was pointing to what was obviously hidden inside her, waiting to be recognized and helped to find its way out. This is how He sees His people. This is how He calls forth the light from within the darkest of appearances. This is how we must learn to see as we encounter people in mission—our purpose is to help their light emerge from within their outer covering.

Next, Jesus and I stopped once more after only a couple steps, like a long journey of His perspective condensed into my little world. Isn't it wonderful how Jesus meets us on our level? Anyway, His next instruction was, *"Listen. Listen to them, and listen to Me."* It sounds so simple, yet there is so much power still to be tapped into through listening. When we take the time to listen to others and hear their story, we give them a form of value that is often beyond what we can offer with our words or ministries. When we jump at an opportunity too quickly we often miss a big part of the story and respond to only part of the need. But when we stop and take the time to listen we begin to process from a higher perspective. A friend once shared a post of a photo on social media of a man who had set up somewhat of a stand or booth on the street. He had a sign that read, "Will pay you $1 to hear your story." What an amazing idea! Instead of simply giving to the poor around him, he was paying them to get to listen to their story and hear their heart. I guarantee he had far greater impact than will ever be able to be measured on earth.

But the second facet is listening to God. We've addressed this principle already, and will address it more in depth in the next chapter, but keeping the ears of our heart open to the voice of the Lord while in mission is paramount to learning to join Him where He is moving. That's how we get to join Him in His interruptions. It's how we get clued in to the compassion of His heart and where His love is on the move. It's how He can give us those gentle nudges of direction to plant seeds in the right soil. Jesus' heart was always tuned in to the Father as He walked and lived out His mission here on earth; it's the only way to stay in alignment with where, or how, God is moving. In mission, no matter how intense or busy the moment might be, we must always have a listening heart tilted towards Him.

Lastly, at the end our walk in my living room, Jesus turned to face me and put both hands on my shoulders, clearly having something very important to say. *"Love them, love them, love them,"* He said, simply and determinedly. I prayed about the intent

I heard and felt from Him, even more than the words. Essentially, what I gleaned from this statement was this: "When you minister to people, they might get loved. But when you love them, they always get ministered to." This may sound like semantics to some, but there really is a powerful difference that comes out of the motives of the heart. Jesus' motivation was always love, not ministry. He didn't come to do ministry and do it more effectively, but to give life and give it more abundantly. There is a huge difference! We can do ministry without love as our engine, but we can't love someone without God accomplishing more ministry than we can fathom.

For this chapter, that's where we'll end. If you hold on to anything from this chapter on embracing the Son in mission I hope you grab this: Wherever you go, whatever you do, *"Love them, love them, love them."*

Moving Forward:

1. Describe the path of Isaiah 58 and what it might look like as you take steps in mission.

2. What does it mean to see as He sees? Discuss the image of seeing someone in whom God's light is trying to break forth from within.

3. What does it mean to listen while walking in mission? Talk about both forms of listening in mission.

4. What does it mean to our mission to simply, but powerfully, *"Love them, love them, love them"*?

End Notes:

1. *Amazing Grace*. DVD, directed by Michael Apted, 2006 (Los Angeles, CA: 20th Century Fox Home Entertainment, 2007).

CHAPTER 4:

THE SPIRIT IN MISSION

The greatest proof of our weakness these days is that there is no longer anything terrible or mysterious about us. . . . The Church has been explained—the surest evidence of her fall. We now have little that cannot be accounted for by psychology and statistics. In that early church they met together on Solomon's porch, and so great was the sense of God's presence that "no man durst join himself to them." The world saw fire in that bush and stood back in fear; but no one is afraid of ashes. Today they dare come as close as they please. They even slap the professed bride of Christ on the back and get coarsely familiar. If we ever again impress unsaved men with a wholesome fear of the supernatural we must have once more the dignity of the Holy Spirit; we must know again that awe-inspiring mystery which comes upon men and churches when they are full of the power of God.

—A.W. Tozer, *Paths to Power*[1]

Part 1: Disciples of the Spirit

Almost all of us would follow Jesus, the Son, into mission of any kind—whether outside our experience or not. But too few of us will follow the Holy Spirit with as much confidence. Why is that? How often do we leave the Spirit out of His vital and ongoing place in mission? Have you noticed that often we even elevate the Bible to a place of greater esteem and sure-fire trust than we do the Spirit of God? As much as I value the Bible, its seen and tangible nature do not give it prevalence over the Spirit. When we embrace the Spirit fully as our Leader, our mission and the people we're called to reach are sure to benefit. Where we place our trust creates quite a statement, whether we realize it or not. I love and cherish the Word of God—*I depend on it*. But even the Bible is not to be depended on more than a living member of the God Head. The Word is sharper than any two-edged sword and *must* be taken with us into mission. But I do not want to pick up that sword and use it to the best of *my* ability, for the Spirit is the One Who teaches us to wield such a sword, and we must become "one" with Him in mission for the Word to be maximized through our lives in mission.

One interesting note I take regarding the Spirit is that the Bible itself tells us there is only one unpardonable sin; do you know what that is? The only unpardonable sin according to Love Himself is blasphemy against the Holy Spirit (see Mark 3:29). Many try to use this verse to invoke fear. Many of us even feel fear when thinking about it, wondering and worrying if we have ever committed this sin ourselves. But I like to look at it another way. I like to flip that passage and see it from the other perspective. If the worst thing we could ever do is blaspheme or dishonor the Holy Spirit, that should show us what a huge value God places on our honor of the Spirit, shouldn't it? What should that truth tell us about the honor due the Spirit from our lives? You would think it would remind us to revere and honor the Holy Spirit even more, right? But even when we do honor the Spirit it is usually more with our lips than our lives or actions. Again, why is this?

If you ask me, it's because the Spirit is unseen, the least tangible yet the most indwelling part of God in our lives. To me, this just doesn't compute. I think there is more opportunity for us to follow and trust the Spirit into unknown territory, and I think this is vital if we will ever see His kingdom truly revealed here on earth as it is in heaven. Mission will be transformed when we will learn to cede control and place full confidence in the Spirit's ability to purposefully and powerfully lead us beyond ways that *we are* comfortable with, and into ways of life and mission that are only possible with God. Walking with the Spirit in mission requires us to see things differently so that the world can see them differently, too, through us.

There's a series of questions I often ask a group when speaking on this subject. I begin by asking: If you could have been alive during Jesus' time to witness Him in action, would you have wanted to be part of it? Without hesitation the answer is always yes, even if the only sign is people very clearly beginning to perk up at the very thought. And I agree—I would, too! And what about the multitudes? Would you have wanted to be in the multitudes who gathered around Him at those special times we reflect back on, like when he fed the five thousand, or stood up for the woman caught in adultery daring anyone without sin to cast the first stone? I would! And I get a pretty strong consensus of the same anytime I pose that question. Most anyone would have loved to have been present for those famous miracles, even if only in the bleachers! Can you imagine the stories we would tell, how we would relay to others what happened in those moments? I've got to believe we'd recollect on His nearness, focus on God's power being manifested, and be in awe of the unseen coming to life! Who wouldn't, right?

What if you could have been one of the recipients of Jesus' touch, and the miracles created from His hand being placed upon you? What if you could have been the woman who reached out by faith to touch the hem of His garment and felt His power literally invade your body, or if you could have been the centurion who received a miracle for someone close to you just by Jesus' speaking a word of faith? I can only imagine how many of us would line up to say "yes" and celebrate the idea of being so near to Jesus that we could receive His touch for us or a loved one.

And what if I told you that you were invited to be one of His twelve disciples? Would you say yes? Would you want to wake up every day and follow His steps through the unique, never previously ventured paths of mission that Jesus paved? Would you follow Him even when it didn't make sense to your understanding? Hands always fly up on that one, everyone willing to volunteer to be one of those few, never questioning the faith it would require knowing they'd be with Jesus Himself. If given this chance today, people would line up across nations to be given such an immense privilege.

But all this only leaves me to ask: *Why do we not do the same today?* Even the disciples, the closest followers of Jesus, only had a 12:1 ratio of discipleship. We may not have Jesus physically present with us today the same way He was in the gospels, but that's why He sent the Holy Spirit—Who is now *indwelling* every believer! Do you know what that means? The Holy Spirit, a very equal part of the God Head with Jesus and the Father, is present with us each day, a 1:1 ratio, far closer than even the disciples had. He is present and waiting to lead us, teach us and disciple us in just the same way. So why do we not view such a miraculous relationship with more joy or give it more esteem? Just because He is unseen, does that make Him any less real?

If you were to wake up tomorrow morning to find Jesus standing at the foot of your bed, saying: *"C'mon, let's go, follow Me today,"* you would say yes! You would abandon the day's plans and agenda and you would follow Him no matter what it looked like. Yet, the Holy Spirit is at least this present every single day of our new lives in Christ. He waits for us to hear Him, to trust Him and to follow Him forward in His ways. We have been given a personal one-on-one Helper Who lives in us, but because He is our *Unseen Leader* we give Him more lip service than we do life, trust or action. Why do we not honor the Holy Spirit the same way we do Jesus? He is no less deserving, and He is every bit and even more present to each of us, just as Jesus was to His disciples.

> *"But you shall receive power when the Holy Spirit has come upon you; and you shall be witnesses to Me in Jerusalem, and in all Judea and Samaria, and to the end of the earth." (Acts 1:8)*

I don't know about you, but this sounds to me like the Holy Spirit is supposed to be the One Who actually leads us into true mission. And yet, we often hold our distance from the very One sent to revolutionize what we are working to improve. Why would I not submit myself freshly each day to His leading and discipleship? Why would I not commit my time and faith to knowing Him as intimately in His unseen ways as I would—or do—Jesus? The Holy Spirit is ready each day to turn every part of our lives into mission with Him, to empower us into the fullness of our calling to the ends of the earth. The question is: *Will we let Him?*

I want to say this clearly, and I say it as much to myself as anyone: There is absolutely no way to *fully* live out our mission, purpose and calling with God apart from surrendering to the daily leadership and empowerment of the Holy Spirit. We might be able to still do works in His name, or carry out parts of our calling; but if we desire to fulfill *everything* we've been created for and leave *nothing* on the table then we must once again recognize and honor the Holy Spirit's place in our lives and mission. I don't want to leave anything on the table. When I stand before God in heaven someday, I want to know that I fully allowed Him to maximize my life and calling for everything He purposed unto Jerusalem, Judea, Samaria and to the ends of the earth. While *I* cannot do this on my own—the Holy Spirit can. A.W. Tozer says it so well in the passage quoted at the opening of this chapter; I think it's worth another look:

The greatest proof of our weakness these days is that there is no longer anything terrible or mysterious about us. . . . The Church has been explained—the surest evidence of her fall. We now have little that cannot be accounted for by psychology and statistics. In that early church they met together on Solomon's porch, and so great was the sense of God's presence that "no man durst join himself to them." The world saw fire in that bush and stood back in fear; but no one is afraid of ashes. Today they dare come as close as they please. They even slap the professed bride of Christ on the back and get coarsely familiar. If we ever again impress unsaved men with a wholesome fear of the supernatural we must have once more the dignity of the Holy Spirit; we must know again that awe-inspiring mystery which comes upon men and churches when they are full of the power of God.

We wake up each day to the Holy Spirit's presence in our lives, to His invitation awakening not only our bodies but seeking also to open the eyes of our hearts to His leading and unplug our spiritual ears to the whispers of His voice. Will we give Him the same esteem we would if waking to Jesus by our side? Will we seek to live through eyes that recognize and honor the Spirit more than we honor what is seen? Will we become disciples of the Spirit? Jesus commissioned His disciples to go and makes disciples of all nations, baptizing them in the name of the Father, the Son and the Holy Spirit. I cannot merely be a disciple of yesterday's teaching and be able to join God where He is moving today. If that were true, Jesus would have only pointed to the Bible as our way to be empowered in mission to the nations. Instead, the last thing Jesus did in Acts 1:8, just before He ascended to heaven, was to say that true mission would begin when the Holy Spirit came upon the disciples. Those of us who have a heart for mission must also be yielded to the same.

Moving Forward:

1. What might it look like to be a disciple of the Spirit?

2. What do you think about the honor we show the Holy Spirit? Do you think we honor Him the same way as the other two members of the Trinity, the Father and the Son? Why? Why not?

3. Re-read the passage from Tozer again. In your own words, what is he communicating? How might it be relevant to your life in mission?

Part 2: The Eyes of the Heart

For we walk by faith, not by sight. (2 Corinthians 5:7)

When I was about eighteen years old I was in a place with God in which I was desperate to know Him beyond my own human limitations. I didn't—*and still don't*—want to see life, people or mission only through my eyes. I knew that I needed something different. I knew that I needed new eyes. I saw there was no way I could live out the calling God created me for unless I lived without the blindness that my own perspective often caused. One of my chief prayers of that season had me longing for God to open the eyes of my heart, realizing I could put more trust in what those eyes saw than in what my physical eyes showed me. You can imagine my elation then when the popular song, "Open the Eyes of My Heart,"[2] came out a couple years later. But that's just it, truths and prayers such as these have to go far deeper than our words, songs and mouths; we have to commit to living them in very real ways. We are the ones, through faith, who help the ways of God to be seen by the world. We prove the Spirit's reality through our trust in Him and willingness to let Him be seen. The world won't trust Him without sight unless we as believers do first. We have to choose to live by such eyes of faith in order to join the Lord in the ways of mission He is moving and beckoning us towards. For our calling to be empowered to its fullest possibilities by the Spirit, new eyes will be needed—and we have to intentionally choose to use them day after day.

For me, this journey spiked to a new level with one specific choice during that season of my life. I went on somewhat of an unusual fast—okay, a very unusual fast: refraining from wearing sunglasses for one year. For further context, you've got to know this was not as easy as it may sound. I lived between California and Colorado, two of the sunniest states in the U.S. And I had recently been given very nice, expensive sunglasses. As part of the fast, I gave them away. Also, you've got to know I was under no misconception that the act of refusing to wear sunglasses would physically change my sight. It was a symbolic act, as many fasts are, that helped lead in a different and renewed direction. By not wearing sunglasses I was reminding myself each day that I would not allow anything to shade or darken my vision. It was a reminder of how purely I had to see without the world's filters if I was going to see *with* the Lord, and not through my flesh. It's so easy to mix the two. We so commonly determine that we are seeing correctly because of applying biblical principles, while at the same time filtering these principles through our own perspectives. But when we see from the eyes of our heart, with God, we determine to see through His filters of unconditional love rather than through our good intentions. This fast was a journey, each day declaring to the Lord my surrender to His eyes and my own need to depend on His vision. To this day, it has dramatically changed the way I see life, the way I see people, and the way I see mission. It took me further away from depending on self and my own perspectives and launched me into a place where the Spirit could show me how He was prepared to move.

And He said to me, "My grace is sufficient for you, for My strength is made perfect in weakness." Therefore most gladly I will rather boast in my infirmities, that the power of Christ may rest upon me. (2 Corinthians 12:9)

"Seeing is believing" is a cultural statement that has wormed its way too far into the ways in which we join the Lord in life or mission. It's a huge part of why it can be such a struggle to honor and be led by the Spirit into the fullness of where He is going and how He is moving. We often look at the idea of not seeing something with our eyes as a weakness to fear. However, this is the sort of weakness we're actually called to embrace, because this is where His grace is proven sufficient and His strength made perfect—*in our weakness.* To surrender our eyes and our right to sight only gives God that much more of an opportunity to make that place His strength in our lives. By making ourselves weak in this way, we empower the Spirit to make us even stronger, and we give Him ripe soil where the power of Christ can actually rest and take root. Wouldn't this be a great place to start as we go forward in mission? Yet, it's so easy to operate by *our* strengths and hold onto our own ways, all the while missing out on the very thing that—the very Person Who—will empower us most.

Paul is a great example in the struggles that he bore with his natural eyes, and in the wrong form of mission he previously had lived out, supposedly *for* God, before this change in his sight began to occur. Paul couldn't recognize the new thing God was doing through Jesus; he was closed to what he couldn't see. It wasn't until his eyes were blinded in the natural that he began to see the true mission and calling God had placed before him in the Spirit. What would we be missing if Paul had continued to live by the intentions of his sight rather than allowing the intangibility of God's unseen power to rest upon him in his weaknesses? And it's not always as extreme as the direction in which Paul was going, either. Often it's as simple as allowing good to be the worst enemy of best. Neither my eyes nor my sunglasses were causing me any problems at all when I began that fast. However, I realized there was something better to be had. I realized I could take that "good" part of my life and exchange it for *His best*, making myself weak so that He could come through that part of my life and make me even stronger. The Holy Spirit is waiting for us to accept this invitation. It all goes back to the power of surrender. I have to see His ways as greater than mine. I have to trust the Spirit to help me more than I can do so for myself—*or others*. I have to believe the Spirit to be more in control than I ever could be, and to know that His love for those I'm reaching out to is far stronger than mine. Just because the Spirit is unseen does not make such dependence a weakness. Paul reminds us from his own experience that it could become our greatest strength.

There's a story of Elisha and his servant fully engaged in mission, and from all human sight they were in serious trouble—that is, until spiritual eyes were opened.

And when the servant of the man of God arose early and went out, there was an army, surrounding the city with horses and chariots. And his servant said to him, "Alas, my master! What shall we do?"

So he answered, "Do not fear, for those who are with us are more than those who are with them."

And Elisha prayed, and said, "Lord, I pray, open his eyes that he may see." Then the Lord opened the eyes of the young man, and he saw. And behold, the mountain was full of horses and chariots of fire all around Elisha.

So when the Syrians came down to him, Elisha prayed to the Lord, and said, "Strike this people, I pray, with blindness." And He struck them with blindness according to the word of Elisha. (2 Kings 6:15-18)

God was already doing more than Elisha's servant had any clue of. Elisha knew that if only his servant's eyes were opened, he, too, could see God's plans over man's. How often might this be the case for us as well? How often might the Spirit be trying to nudge our hearts to see the table He has already set, while we run about worrying where on earth everyone is going to sit? How often do we go forward, blind to the ways in which God is present and ready, instead consumed with worry and fear about what will happen?

The Spirit is always moving in big and small ways, and while we often ask God to accomplish the task *we* are staring at, it's the Holy Spirit who is patiently waiting for us to *join Him in His mission*. We are too often blind to the very answer we are waiting for—not to mention the parts we don't know that God will surprise us with! There is an unseen playing field we're afraid to join. We'd rather go over plays and statistics in safety on the sidelines without fear of running out of bounds. That's okay I suppose, as long as we remember that the sidelines are already out of bounds as well. From where we currently sit—or see—we cannot accomplish all that God is ready to do. We cannot join the Father in His fullest form of mission without recognizing the Spirit's greater role, and allowing Him to call the plays.

Most of our fear of surrendering to the Spirit in mission comes from a lack of perspective, or, perhaps just too full a dose of our own perspective. New is scary for many of us. And, unfortunately, trusting the Holy Spirit is scary for many of us, too. But such fear has never caused any growth, nor does it bear fruit. Such fear actually strangles the fullness of mission that could be possible through our lives, whereas the Spirit launches us with Him into even more abundant mission. We won't find His new ways while using our old eyes. Just ask Paul.

> *And Ananias went his way and entered the house; and laying his hands on him he said, "Brother Saul, the Lord Jesus, who appeared to you on the road as you came, has sent me that you may receive your sight and be filled with the Holy Spirit."*
>
> *Immediately there fell from his eyes something like scales, and he received his sight at once; and he arose and was baptized. (Acts 9:17-18)*

The primary reason we do not allow the Spirit more room to lead us in daily life and mission the way we might Jesus is because He is unseen to our physical eyes. And yet, according to Jesus, the Spirit's presence in and upon our lives is actually where mission begins. We cannot remain trapped between these two differing cultures of perspective. The fullness of what God made available can't be realized as such. Will we let go of our trust in a sight that can paradoxically blind us and instead allow the Holy Spirit to open our eyes to what He sees? Will we cease from excusing our fear of trusting the Holy Spirit as anything but? We are afraid only because we haven't allowed faith's eyes to see—yet. The answer isn't found in staying on the sidelines, avoiding participating in the Spirit's ways; the answer is found in reviving our eyes of faith rather than trusting in physical sight. Our mission cannot be completed, or even begun, apart from honoring the Spirit and embracing His vital role in our lives. How do we depend on the Spirit's leading? Well, we may need to trade in our eyes that "see" for eyes that first believe.

Moving Forward:

1. How do you currently allow sight—or lack thereof—to dictate your reliance on the Holy Spirit?

2. How can we learn from Paul's journey from sight to Spirit?

3. What unspoken fears or insecurities might be present in your life that make you want to keep your eyes open and depend on sight rather than being led "blindly" by the Spirit of God? How do you need to surrender those fears?

Part 3: Where Mission Begins

The disciples were commissioned to go out into mission in the gospels (Matthew 28:19). But it wasn't until the Spirit came that they were equipped and empowered to *actually* go (Acts 1:8). If we are going to change or strengthen the way we do mission, it will largely happen by changing the place in our lives where mission begins. Mission is a calling much greater than our external actions; it's joining the heart of the Father towards His worldwide family. That's why He sent His Son, and that's why His Son sent His Spirit. Now, His Spirit sends and empowers us. I believe, for us, the Holy Spirit is where mission begins.

We looked at this subject in part one, going over Jesus' last words before He ascended to heaven.

"But you shall receive power when the Holy Spirit has come upon you; and you shall be witnesses to Me in Jerusalem, and in all Judea and Samaria, and to the end of the earth." (Acts 1:8)

Jesus told His disciples to get ready, as mission was about to change by the presence of the Holy Spirit, and as a result, they were going to be sent out like never before. It was in Acts 2, at Pentecost, that the Spirit came, and the dynamics of how the believers lived, how they preached and how they multiplied began to change. But for me, I have always felt a great affinity for another time, when they were gathered together in an "upper room," in Acts 4:31-34. For me, this is when their mission was actually launched, and the results were anything but typical.

And when they had prayed, the place where they were assembled together was shaken; and they were all filled with the Holy Spirit, and they spoke the word of God with boldness. Now the multitude of those who believed were of one heart and one soul; neither did anyone say that any of the things he possessed was his own, but they had all things in common. And with great power the apostles gave witness to the resurrection of the Lord Jesus. And great grace was upon them all. Nor was there anyone among them who lacked.... (Acts 4:31-34)

I always go back to this passage when I think of where modern missions began. There are so many parts that astound me, and I don't have space to go into them all. (I've addressed it further in a prior book, *The Power of Uncommon Unity: Becoming the Answer to Jesus' Final Prayer*,[3] if you'd like to read further.) In this passage, the Holy Spirit came upon them as they sought God's ways of mission in prayer, and the Spirit upped the ante, it seems, on how they moved forward. They didn't just speak the word of God, but they spoke it with greater boldness. They didn't just gather together, but they were of "one heart and one soul," which means they were "in sync or in tune" and "breathing spiritually together" as the Greek defines it. That's a depth of oneness that doesn't come simply from proximity to one another or natural agreement; this special oneness was only now made possible because of the Spirit's presence in their lives. Their new hearts, within each of their renewed lives, were now all beating as one, united by Him Who was within them, and Who was leading them. They didn't just walk in grace, but in *great grace*, and not only did they go out as witnesses, they went out with *great power* as witnesses of Jesus' resurrection, just as Jesus had said would happen. And perhaps my favorite part, one that always blows my mind: *"Nor was there anyone among them who lacked."*

Do you realize what that just said? They were empowered by the Holy Spirit into a form of bold mission, one that enabled them to give extravagantly because of the great grace they were walking in, and despite their generous giving it says that there wasn't anyone among them who had any lack. Poverty among them was eradicated! Is that not one of our primary goals in our current format of mission, to go and solve poverty or at least help those in poverty? But here we see a testimony of poverty being wiped out. I can't help but be drawn to look at the source of that testimony. I can't just try and copy the action or the result for real change to happen; I have to go back to the root. I must go back to understand that for this group of apostles, their mission wasn't determined merely by what they did or what they had in their hands; if it had been, they would have run out. Their dramatic result came to fruition because all that they "did" or "had" in mission sprang from a source greater than their own hopes, desires or ways. Their gifts, abilities, good intentions and what they had in their hands to give were multiplied because the Spirit was fueling their mission. Why do we not more greatly emphasize this today? What might the possibilities be if we did?

If we want to see poverty eradicated, why do we not more often go back to the Source and realize the Spirit is waiting to empower us further, into greater mission than we can accomplish among the most rich or gifted? We are not held back by a lack of resources, but rather by a lack of dependence on the Spirit, Who is in the business of multiplying resources! I've often heard mentioned how much more we could accomplish in mission if people just gave more and weren't so selfish with the excess they have. There is great truth in that. But you know what? It goes beyond that. I don't care if we could convince every wealthy person in the world to join our mission—if we aren't living it out from the right source, it'll still eventually become a well that runs dry! We don't merely need more money to accomplish what God has set before us around the world; we need more of the Holy Spirit! We need to go back to our own "upper rooms" and begin mission from there. We need to go to that Source in our own personal time, and we need to go there together as teams or churches launching out together. The mission that's already been commissioned cannot be accomplished if we do not more fully rely on the empowerment of the Holy Spirit.

So much time is spent searching for resources to change the world, and yet, too often we ignore the Greatest Resource, sent by Christ to dwell within us. Well, let's let Him out of us! The upper room where this group gathered was the launching place of mission, and they left behind a testimony, a baton for us to pick up and run with. The book of Acts is not merely a history book for how the twelve disciples were called to walk: It is a testimony of Jesus Christ lived out to the world through their lives by the empowerment of the Holy Spirit. When will we pick up this testimony? When will we once again value Whom we meet within the upper room? When will God's power be allowed back in to Christian mission? We only need look back to where mission began. Can you tell I'm passionate about the subject? As much as anything, I'm passionate about the possibilities that will come to life when we allow mission to be empowered in this way—*through all our lives!*

Perhaps you've felt a commissioning, yet you can't figure out why you haven't been launched or sent out to begin your mission. Perhaps in your gut you sense that more is possible, but you haven't known how, or where, to begin. Perhaps the Holy Spirit is awaiting your attention. Perhaps there is an upper room He is waiting to meet you in, a place to equip you, and a greater connection from which to empower you in new ways. Where is your upper room? Do you have one? Or, *where was it?* Do you ever return there to be renewed? If you had one, has it faded away? Or, maybe this is your invitation to discover one for the first time, as well as all the purposes God may birth from there. Perhaps God is ready to launch you into a new season of life and mission, but not just the mission you might accomplish with good intentions or effective methods—I'm talking about the kind of mission the disciples learned in the book of Acts, the kind of mission that is far beyond the limitations of self and that therefore bears impossible fruit, the kind that remains!

My "upper room" was actually a basement bedroom I lived in for 3 years between the ages of seventeen and twenty, just before Destiny and I were married. Whenever I think about the mission God has led, or is leading us in, for me, it all goes back to that unforgettable place and the times with Him. Trainings, books, manuals, schools—all these can be very *good* things. But none can replace our own upper room where the Holy Spirit is given time and space to invade our lives and prepare us for launch.

I would shut all the doors, load up the five-disc player with hours of worship music and get lost in His presence. Sometimes it would be so hard to peel myself out of the depths of God's heart. The room became saturated with God's presence, like a misty rainforest, and my whole being was revived. I would lie there before the Lord for hours, rarely even talking much—more listening, to be honest—sometimes worshiping, just wanting to know Him more and learn His ways above my own. In that basement, the Holy Spirit became a real and tangible mentor in my life, so much so that physical sight became very low on my priority list during our interactions. My heart knew Him, which opened new eyes. Even starting to think back to these times moves me near to tears. I would dream with God, and I felt like He shared His dreams with me, with gentle, hope-filled nudges of the heart. He gave me vision I wouldn't have otherwise had, love that was greater than my own, understanding that was beyond my own reason. The Holy Spirit broke every box I had tried to place Him in during our times together and prepared me for all kinds of mission I wouldn't have otherwise known. Those were special times I could never replace, and I'll never be the same because of them. Those "upper room" times shaped the journey my life has taken and the way I've learned to walk with the Lord. I can still taste what He and I shared together during those times dining at His table.

There was one specific request that I did pray day after day. I didn't know what I was asking at first, just that I wanted more. Yet I realized that in my own human terms, I couldn't even begin to categorize what "more" looked like. So I began to ask: *"Lord, teach me the things that I don't even know how to ask for."* I now consider this prayer, outside of believing on the Lord Jesus Christ, to be one of the most powerful I've ever learned to utter. Even now, I pray I will never grow so content or so full of myself that I stop uttering those necessary words, allowing the Spirit to expand my territory beyond what I know to ask for—beyond what I can cognitively think or imagine. The Holy Spirit is not limited by my experience or education the way I am. Therefore my dependence doesn't lessen, it only grows.

I try to recreate that "upper room" season at times, and different times of my life bring different versions as I am renewed, but nothing replaces those times and that season where the Spirit soaked me like a sponge with Himself. I was drenched in His presence, and that season became the launching pad from which I was empowered to join the Lord moving forward. I didn't know it at the time, but the Holy Spirit was already designing inside me a greater form of mission before I could ever walk in it. He was simply awaiting my time and permission to show me.

I often refer to those seasons in our lives as a "wilderness of oneness." Sometimes it's a lonely season, or a tough one, or perhaps it's actually a season specially chosen by the Lord Himself. Maybe it was a time you had to surrender something you wanted to hold onto; thus, it felt like a wilderness. Though to God, it's anything but. To Him it's a place of oneness where He can now empower your commissioning to come to life in ways you wouldn't have dreamed of before. It's where mission starts to flow through His engine rather than our own.

To me, these seasons relate to the journey of a caterpillar becoming a butterfly. The first goes about life and mission scooting and crawling, the other flutters through the skies, from flower to tree, upon wings that had been deep inside the entire time. What is the difference? What happened in between? The cocoon happened. We talk so much of the two creatures on either side of metamorphosis, but we rarely talk about the time in between. But this cocoon time, this is where the Spirit empowers us—*this is where we are launched from!* The cocoon is our upper room, where a whole new world opens up that our eyes couldn't perceive previously. And suddenly, mission looks a lot different from the sky than from the scooting nature that once called for striving amid limited vision. We must ask ourselves, are we living Christ's mission from the perspective of the caterpillar, or through the new nature of the butterfly? If mission for us is still characterized by a lot of scooting, striving and insecurity, trying to measure up and not get squashed by others, then perhaps the some cocoon time is what we really need. Many of us avoid that cocoon because we already feel that since we're going too slow or are too insignificant, we can't afford to lose time or opportunity. But the cocoon is actually a multiplier, a place of launch that goes far beyond what was surrendered while tucked within it.

Mission begins in the "upper room." It begins in your personal cocoon with your Creator, getting to know the new ways the Spirit is equipping you for, the new mission into which He will propel you and others. This kind of surrender to the Spirit opens up new vistas and will become that place you look back on and say, *"That's where true mission began."*

Moving Forward:

1. Why would we want to copy the root of mission rather than only the external actions or fruit? Discuss the powerful fruit that came out of the root of the disciples' mission.

2. How might mission look different for you personally if it began from the same root in the Holy Spirit as it did for those in the book of Acts?

3. Do you have an "upper room" from the past or present, or will you perhaps in the very near future? What does/might that look like? How will you help yourself stay committed to returning to such a counter-cultural, but necessary place?

Part 4: The "Jericho Strategy"

As we join the Spirit in mission, I actually believe the act of listening takes over for our usual dependence on the sight our eyes provide. This is a listening of our hearts to that often still, small voice of the Spirit. His voice becomes more real to us the more we yield our rushed actions to Him in the stillness from which His mission often originates.

In church circles, we know the story as "Joshua and the Battle of Jericho." I've personally come to know this as the "Jericho Strategy" because as a completely unique approach to a God-given mission, it has helped me to see my need to be completely reliant on listening to God.

We often remember the walls crashing down in miraculous fashion, but I think we often forget to look at how exactly Joshua and the Israelites set course on such an "outside the box" mission. What ended with such a loud shout and crashing walls actually began with quiet listening. We can easily forget the realities that could have been present, or take for granted where Joshua placed his priorities in order to see God's promise come to life. Often times, we will receive a prompting from God, a calling, an open door to begin mission, etc. However, almost nearly as often we will take what God has given and go about it or finish it according to natural ways of mission that *we* are accustomed to. But we wouldn't have that famous victory to look back on at Jericho if Joshua hadn't gone about his mission in a way very different than how we conduct most mission strategies today. We like to enjoy fruit, but too rarely do we go back to the source to see the unique or extraordinary root that fruit was birthed *from*. That's what perspective is all about, going back to the root view and learning to live mission from there. If and when we do, perhaps we, too, will see God bring extraordinary results from very simple acts of faith and obedience. It all starts with our commitment to listening to the Spirit of God as a vital part of our commitment to God's mission.

Look at how Joshua began. He was given a promise; God said He would give Jericho into the Israelites' hands. It would have been so easy to move forward in natural ways and expect God to deliver a supernatural result. But Joshua recognized the unique ways of God, that His ways are higher—*and different*—than our ways. He didn't try to achieve through the ways of the flesh what obviously began in the Spirit. Rather, Joshua understood that he had to keep the mission flowing directly from God's capabilities rather than his own. So, Joshua's strategy began with listening to unlikely orders.

> *And it came to pass, when Joshua was by Jericho, that he lifted his eyes and looked, and behold, a Man stood opposite him with His sword drawn in His hand. And Joshua went to Him and said to Him, "Are you for us or for our adversaries?" So He said, "No, but as Commander of the army of the Lord I have now come." And Joshua fell on his face to the earth and worshiped, and said to Him, "What does my Lord say to His servant?" Then the Commander of the Lord's army said to Joshua, "Take your sandal off your foot, for the place where you stand is holy." And Joshua did so. (Joshua 5:13-15)*

"What does my Lord say to His servant?" What a way to start a mission—to inquire of the Lord! I hope and pray I never begin anything as precious to God's heart as mission without inquiring directly of Him. I need His strategy more than my own intentions or efforts. I need to know the nooks and crannies of the ways of the Spirit that He wants to lead me through. He has a victory that He might make known, but His ways of getting there are usually so different than ours. Joshua recognized the "Commander of the Lord's" mission and knew there was a higher, different way to be discovered—and all he had to do was ask.

And the Lord said to Joshua: "See! I have given Jericho into your hand, its king, and the mighty men of valor. You shall march around the city, all you men of war; you shall go all around the city once. This you shall do six days. And seven priests shall bear seven trumpets of rams' horns before the ark. But the seventh day you shall march around the city seven times, and the priests shall blow the trumpets.

"It shall come to pass, when they make a long blast with the ram's horn, and when you hear the sound of the trumpet, that all the people shall shout with a great shout; then the wall of the city will fall down flat. And the people shall go up every man straight before him." (Joshua 6:2-5)

Unfortunately, our human or natural tendency in mission is to hear something like "Jericho Strategy" and begin to copy the exact external ways in which they conquered Jericho, rather than copying the point of origin that got them there. I'm not calling us back to marching around the grounds we hope to take for the seven days or seven times like the Israelites did; rather I pray we come back to the root strategy—inquiring and listening—that this great testimony of Jericho stems from.

I wonder if many of us would have heard the promise, "I have given Jericho into your hand," and interrupted the rest of the instructions with our zeal to rush into mission? How often might we be cutting the Lord off mid-sentence—after hearing our call or commission—without taking the time to listen to His strategy for how He wants us to join Him as *He* brings the promise to life? How many of us would have moved forward with great ideas, perhaps forming a leadership team, and possibly investigating who had what gifts with which to bring down those walls? *"Oh, you have a pick axe, that's perfect! Ah, your bulldozer will fit right in! A wrecking ball, what a great addition! C'mon on, let's go—we've been promised the victory!"* But that's not what Joshua did, not at all! We could assemble the greatest leadership team in the world and they would *never* come up with the strategy God gave to Joshua to employ at Jericho. Joshua wasn't "doing" mission, he was *joining God* where *He* planned to move. A lot of our great intentions are just that—great intentions. But if we will take the time and patience to listen to God's strategy, our great intentions of mission transform into *simple obedience* within His mission, and they always meet with His success.

Once Joshua heard God's strategy, the people's mission became very simple—obey. Obedience is a term that has perhaps become too boring, something we have segregated from the new, modern form of mission and its rising sex appeal today. But when we prioritize listening to God—inviting the Spirit to lead our mission—obedience takes on a renewed meaning full of powerful possibilities just waiting to unfold.

Obedience calls for us to join God in His fresh plan for the time and creates opportunity within a powerful principle too often ignored—*trust*. When we listen to God, all we have to do is obey. When we obey, and therefore align ourselves with not only His mission, but also His timing, then all that is left for us to do is trust Him with the results—His results.

So the people shouted when the priests blew the trumpets. And it happened when the people heard the sound of the trumpet, and the people shouted with a great shout, that the wall fell down flat. Then the people went up into the city, every man straight before him, and they took the city. (Joshua 6:20)

Mission accomplished! How? It was through trust. One of the greatest "results" of mission in biblical history—or the history of the world for that matter—came about because the people obeyed God and then trusted Him to bring about results they could have only begun to strive for on their own. They lifted their trust more than they even lifted a hand. How's that for redefining mission?

Nothing against lifting a hand in mission, a lot of love can be constructed that way and is quite necessary, but it's only one part of mission. Trust, through listening and obedience, is an underrated power God is waiting for us to partner with Him in more often.

This is the "Jericho Strategy." It's not as extravagant as it sounds; it's rather simple, actually: *Listen, obey, trust.* Take the time and feed the desire to go directly to the Source, inquire of Him and listen for His ways. Step forward in obedience to join Him in His mission, and then trust God with the rest, allowing Him room to move in the fullness of His love through you. What we are really doing is putting our trust in God's capabilities and love within mission over our own.

Moving Forward:

1. What is the difference in mission between moving out of our own good intentions and yielding to first inquire of the Lord? Why is this important?

2. How might such trust in God affect the "results" or fruit from your life and mission? Why?

3. How could you employ the "Jericho Strategy" in your life and mission?

End Notes:

1. A.W. Tozer, *Paths to Power* (London, Oliphants Ltd., 1964)
2. Paul Baloche, "Open the Eyes of My Heart," from the album *Open the Eyes of My Heart,* copyright © 2000 by Integrity Music - 17862, audio CD.
3. Joey LeTourneau, *The Power of Uncommon Unity: Becoming the Answer to Jesus' Final Prayer* (Shippensburg, PA: Destiny Image Publishers, 2013).

CHAPTER 5:

OUR POVERTY IN MISSION

Part 1: Stolen Vision

Where there is no vision, the people perish. . . . (Proverbs 29:18, KJV)

If people can't see what God is doing, they stumble all over themselves; but when they attend to what He reveals, they are most blessed. (Proverbs 29:18, The Message[1])

Most often, we cultivate mission to address the poverty of others. But until we address our own poverty, we will continue to live out a watered-down version of mission. One of the primary culprits keeping us from joining God in His ways of mission is *our* poverty. It might sound almost wrong to deal with our poverty before other more obvious areas of poverty in the world. But how can we effectively transform the poverty of others when looking at their situation through the lens of our own different version of poverty? Whether we initially realize it or not, when we launch out into mission we often carry along as much poverty as those we are going to help—albeit a different kind. While we may travel to a person or a nation whose poverty is external, natural, and easy to recognize, ours is spiritual in nature, a poverty of *belonging* and *self-worth*.

I can see and hear it now, quite vividly actually: Our poverty in mission leads us to envision ourselves out on the field, poverty-stricken children running to us, and we are scooping them up in a slow-motion rescue scene while the chorus, *"Did you ever know that you're my hero?"* sung by Bette Midler[2] plays in the background. We are not likely daydreaming this consciously, but the poverty inside us is probably singing along. Our need to find value and worth is playing itself out through this scene, whether we know it or not. We may never declare it to ourselves cognitively, much less out loud, but there is a poverty within that confirms it as true. Part of us is still trying to earn worth while also genuinely giving it away. There remains a part of us that wants to be a savior, a hero, someone coming to the rescue. We are called to be like Jesus, called to carry our cross and follow Him, called to share and show the gospel and make disciples of the nations; but we don't need to be a savior, nor can we be—there is only One Who can fill this role and it has already been accomplished.

There's a fine line between these two parts of being Christ-like in mission, between being a hero and simply loving like Jesus. There are people all over the world who do need some form of rescue. But first, before we can truly love that child or any other person the way Jesus does, the hurting child *in us* needs to be rescued, re-filled and renewed before we can fully offer the Father's love to others living in poverty. We don't have to be perfect, far from it. It's not about getting all our ducks in a row before we reach out, or step out and go. Instead, it is about joining the Lord out of loving obedience rather than valiant effort. It is about going back to the Lord for perspective so that the fullness of His mission can be felt through our lives. Otherwise, when we live through our own insecurities, out of an internal spiritual poverty, it's very difficult to see correctly, or consistently. It mixes joining

God with fulfilling self, even if in a noble way. Our poverty feeds off theirs, and vice versa.

Our spiritual poverty goes all the way back to the Garden of Eden and original sin. We now know that we don't have to carry this poverty of insecurity through our lives or mission because Jesus has already paid for and conquered it, but that doesn't mean we always leave it behind—and it has more far-reaching effects than we know. Often, this spiritual sort of poverty is the very thing that will fall out of our arms when we truly pick up our cross to follow Him. Following Jesus into His ways of mission—those of joining the Father—is no easy way. It requires us to deny self. But in mission, we not only feed the hungry, we feed our spiritual poverty with their physical poverty, we feed our need to be needed with their need. We can actually feed our self-worth rather than establish theirs, addressing just their bellies instead, keeping the cycle of poverty spinning until the next mealtime rolls around. The people may not be *asking* us to feed more than their bellies, but that doesn't mean there isn't a greater or equivalent need to be recognized at the same time. For those of us in the western world, this has become an unnaturally natural form of mission and way of life. It has become our double vision while we try to join Him in His ways of mission. But it doesn't have to be that way. We don't have to feed the cycle of dependence; we can empower others out of it, and ourselves as well. We can learn to see differently—*and freely*—once again.

> *Then the serpent said to the woman, "You will not surely die. For God knows that in the day you eat of it your eyes will be opened, and you will be like God, knowing good and evil." So when the woman saw that the tree was good for food, that it was pleasant to the eyes, and a tree desirable to make one wise, she took of its fruit and ate. She also gave to her husband with her, and he ate.*
>
> *Then the eyes of both of them were opened, and they knew that they were naked; and they sewed fig leaves together and made themselves coverings. And they heard*

the sound of the Lord God walking in the garden in the cool of the day, and Adam and his wife hid themselves from the presence of the Lord God among the trees of the garden. (Genesis 3:4-8)

In the Garden of Eden, Adam and Eve walked freely with God with a secure and focused purpose. They knew their identity as His children and the mission He had given them: to take dominion over the earth, be fruitful and multiply. All that time, they were naked without being any the wiser. Bottom line, they were free from comparison and the insecurities that stem from it. But the moment they ate that fruit, the second that sin entered, they lost their vision. Before this, they had single vision of God and His purposes for their lives. But after, they couldn't just go forward freely anymore, they wasted time and focus protecting self, clothing their newfound insecurities with fig leaves.

We often focus solely on the sin and disobedience that took place, but do we miss what was stolen in the process? Do we realize that their single-minded, free-hearted vision was taken from them immediately? When Jesus conquered sin and death we know that He finished our salvation and repaired what had been broken between us and God. But do we realize that in redeeming our identity and mission, He restored our vision as well? Do we realize that as believers in the new covenant we can live once again with the single-minded, free-hearted vision that God intended from the beginning? We don't have to try to address our insecurity while also trying to live our purpose. The two don't mix well but rather war against one another. One is a downward perspective of fear and self-protection; the other is a self-surrendered freedom to look upward and return to the unblemished and therefore uncovered identity and role in mission we were created to walk in with God. We can't fully go forward in our purpose if half our purpose is still to protect or fill self. We must let ourselves be freed from this kind of poverty that keeps us feeling naked, fearing lack, wavering with double-mindedness, striving always to cover up and measure up. Christ has given back a freedom that we haven't fully embraced enough. With this freedom comes a vision, away from self, purely focused on God, seeing with Him and joining Him once again in the purposes He has set before us, unhindered by any purpose of the flesh. Jesus didn't just finish sin, He restored the vision we need for our identity and our mission, in order to love the world as purely as He does.

I don't want to overcomplicate things or to add more inward focus on trying to fix self; it's actually quite the opposite. I'm advocating for a return to a greater simplicity of mission—a losing of self, letting ourselves walk freely again without the fig leaves and with nothing to prove, knowing that God has already created us with innate, significant worth from which we are able to fully live and give. When we are trapped in spiritual poverty we tend to function out of *"what we do"* instead of *"who we are."* Often, our mission is a big part of our own search for self-worth. God certainly uses this on our journey, but we have to realize that someone else's poverty is feeding off this version of our own, and we're only making the cycle of dependence spin that much faster, and deeper.

When we break out of our cycles of living or doing mission from insecurity—even a little bit—we also begin to break the straw that stirs the drink. We can't eradicate the poverty of others unless we first address and eradicate our own. In mission, even while feeding the poorest of the poor, we must also take them straight to the Source, to their own direct connection *with* God, not just handing out our recipe but letting them partake of the very same thing we do. That is, after all how Jesus operated. Many people flocked to Him with specific needs and requests, but He so often gave them more than what they asked for, something deeper they couldn't always make sense of in the moment. And they didn't always have to understand the seed He planted in them in order for it still to sprout at its appointed time. Jesus also did evangelism and discipleship at the same time. He didn't separate them the way we often do. He presented a full vision, even when His listeners couldn't comprehend—as was the case with the disciples many times—so that they would not have to settle for a half version of what God was making available through His life. Escape from hell or hunger is only half way; He's created us for more! We bring not merely a survival gospel, but one of empowerment. We can't just dole out survival anymore. If we give people vision for only half way, then that will become their goal and finish line. But if we give them vision beyond survival, even for purposes that may seem too far off or impossible to us considering their current state, we'll restore to them the vision Jesus provided, and then they can be fed as well. We'll cover this part of dealing with poverty in more depth later. I share it now because realizing such vision and possibility is part of our climb out of our own poverty cycle.

From the beginning, our desire must be to lead people away from depending on our ministry, thereby empowering them out of their place of impoverished need. When we take back the vision for our lives and mission that Jesus has already restored, we will naturally have vision to pass on to others from the outset of our interaction. This change in our vision and motives can then begin to lift others out of their poverty. We may not always see the results immediately, but that goes back to our need to trust God after we obey. It's not about the immediate results we can measure in their lives, but about rightly placed seeds that will bear new, nourishing fruit generations beyond what we will ever witness for ourselves. Restoring vision, in parallel with addressing basic physical needs, is a recipe of love that lifts people out of even the greatest poverty over many years as they continue to walk forward—and it becomes what they, too, will pass on. Because next time, they won't be looking for us to come and rescue them out of the pit they've fallen into—their restored vision will have allowed them to use our help as a bridge to cross, or to avoid the pit altogether, because they are now able to see purpose far greater and worth persevering to reach. Their focus won't be survival anymore; they'll have been given a new vision—allowing them to thrive and flourish in the identity and purpose for which they, too, were created.

Moving Forward:

1. What does it mean to battle an internal, spiritual poverty?

2. Have you ever felt this "hero complex" in mission? (It's okay, I have, too.) How can this be hurtful to others, and ourselves, without us even knowing it?

3. How does our poverty impact our ability to wholly love and empower others out of theirs? What is the vision we must take back?

Part 2: Abraham, Sarah, Hagar & Ishmael

Now Sarai, Abram's wife, had borne him no children. And she had an Egyptian maidservant whose name was Hagar. So Sarai said to Abram, "See now, the Lord has restrained me from bearing children. Please, go in to my maid; perhaps I shall obtain children by her." And Abram heeded the voice of Sarai.

Then Sarai, Abram's wife, took Hagar her maid, the Egyptian, and gave her to her husband Abram to be his wife, after Abram had dwelt ten years in the land of Canaan. So he went in to Hagar, and she conceived. And when she saw that she had conceived, her mistress became despised in her eyes.

Then Sarai said to Abram, "My wrong be upon you! I gave my maid into your embrace; and when she saw that she had conceived, I became despised in her eyes. The Lord judge between you and me." So Abram said to Sarai, "Indeed your maid is in your hand; do to her as you please." And when Sarai dealt harshly with her, she fled from her presence.

Now the Angel of the Lord found her by a spring of water in the wilderness, by the spring on the way to Shur. And He said, "Hagar, Sarai's maid, where have you come from, and where are you going?" She said, "I am fleeing from the presence of my mistress Sarai." The Angel of the Lord said to her, "Return to your mistress, and submit yourself under her hand." Then the Angel of the Lord said to her, "I will multiply your descendants exceedingly, so that they shall not be counted for multitude." And the Angel of the Lord said to her: "Behold, you are with child, and you shall bear a son. You shall call his name Ishmael, because the Lord has heard your affliction. He shall be a wild man; his hand shall be against every man, and every man's against him. And he shall dwell in the presence of all his brethren. . . ."

So Hagar bore Abram a son; and Abram named his son, whom Hagar bore, Ishmael. Abram was eighty-six years old when Hagar bore Ishmael to Abram. (Genesis 16: 1-12, 15-16)

Thirteen years before God began to fulfill purpose and promise through Abraham by blessing him and Sarah with Isaac, Abraham's first son, Ishmael, arrived on the scene. However, *this* child was the attempt of Abraham, Sarah and Hagar (for her own different reasons) to fulfill God's promise in their lives for themselves because they were getting impatient waiting for God to establish His promise in His best way and timing. Abraham is known for his unwavering faith and trust in God, as well as the close friendship they shared. Yet even he let go of trust for a time and started his own version of mission while waiting for the fulfillment of the promise. Abraham and Sarah had the right idea in regards to the promise God would fulfill through their lives; but their ways and timing were completely off and were driven out of their own efforts. Before they knew it, their good intentions had birthed life, but with a lot of unnecessary conflict attached.

Abraham was eighty-six years old, after all. If anyone had seemingly earned the right to be impatient, I suppose it was he—if such a right exists. Our poverty in mission often produces impatience that does not align well with God's kingdom being established here on earth. Abraham had been so faithful, in ways few others have ever duplicated, living richly on the inside while waiting for God to bring forth such promises on the outside, too. Eighty-six years! That's how long he had already waited up to this point, and Isaac hadn't yet even been born. That is eighty-six years of trusting God over man, internal over external, strengthening his inner man in the Lord and His nature rather than falling prey to the doubt of circumstance. Abraham has always been the Old Testament person I have looked up to most, because of the inner battles he won every day in order to trust God for His best mission possible. Yet even Abraham had moments amiss. His example should remind us not how perfect we must be, nor of our own freedom (or tendency) to make mistakes, but rather of how important it is in our lives and mission that we stay fresh with God every step of the way, because one rash step out of alignment with God can lead to our devising our own well-reasoned plans and giving birth to a spiritual "Ishmael." We must not measure by man's strength or capabilities nor try to see with his lenses for even a moment.

Have you ever birthed an Ishmael? I have. You may have, too, but just not known it. God still used Ishmael and brought forth abundant fruit from his life because of God's faithfulness to His covenant with Abraham. But it was not the original promise, or mission, that God had planned. Ishmael also brought forth a lot of challenges, challenges that birthed even more challenges. To be clear, in referring to "Ishmael" I'm not focused on a people group or specific descendants of Ishmael. Rather, Ishmael shows us an example in Abraham's life of how we can get ahead of God and conceive something of self that will later war with the true promise that God wants to conceive through us. The Ishmaelites were known to roam the desert, frequently in conflict with others. That's what can happen when we mix God's plans with our application or timing. We might even have the best intentions at heart, but we cannot bring God's promises to earth through our own ways, methods and timing. Trying to execute God's ways through our methods or timing is an example of the age-old picture of oil and water competing against one another, unable to mix. But we're not actually competing against God; we're competing against the reflections of our own internal, spiritual poverty. We see our jar of oil only a quarter full and try to top it off with water. Sometimes it's not even that drastic—we might only allow in a drop of water, but it still separates and causes conflict. We cannot compromise mission by rushing it for the sake of our own ideas or insecurities.

Our partnership with God in mission requires more than action, good deeds or best intentions; it requires ongoing trust. Trust is not faith alone, but faith mixed with patience. God's mission requires patience, an undervalued and power-packed dynamic of the kingdom that isn't as passive as we have deemed it. For having patience while joining God isn't a lack of activity, but is actually a trek of many steps ventured over internal mountain peaks that must be conquered. We have to let God establish His best without intervening and undercutting what He is forming. We rarely do this intentionally, but we birth such "Ishmaels" out of our poverty in mission and a personal "need" to act.

As I mentioned, Abraham is someone I've always looked up to, and this story has always been one of the foundations in my heart as my family and I have sought to walk with God in His ways of mission. But even with such awareness, we saw our own Ishmael birthed simply through misapplying God's promises and getting ahead of Him. As people often do, we felt everything was adding up, and others agreed. Externally things were coming together, our intentions were good, the mission seemed right and truly matched the promises we had been given, but soon we realized this was not an "Isaac" we were carrying, it was our "Ishmael." We had gotten ahead of God, even if only a step or two. We were off in application of God's promises and directives, having moved forward after hearing 75% rather than realizing there was more He was still planning to give us and establish in our hearts before it could be established on earth. It breaks my heart to even think of this, or the conflicts it produced. I just thank God that His grace was, and is, sufficient, and we got back on our previous course, trusting Him for the same promises—this time through His means. It's an amazing thing then when you start to see your real "Isaac" enter the world—it is completely worth the wait!

Rarely do we birth an Ishmael purposefully, or on our own. It usually involves agreement from others who are also operating out of some form of their own spiritual poverty, looking for belonging or worth, too. That's one of the challenges of spiritual poverty— most of us have it and it feeds off of and validates the different versions in one another. That's a very subtle deception that requires us to greatly discern what confirmation is from God and what is from man. It's easy to find people who will agree with something, which leads you to mistake their participation as a confirmation from God. Usually, everyone is looking for identity in different ways, and the "Ishmaels" we may bring about in mission might also give identity, albeit a false one, to those like Hagar who are searching in their own way. As it was with Abraham, Hagar and Sarah, our Ishmaels typically stem from timing and application or identity. Abraham and Sarah missed the timing and application of the promise; and Hagar may have been searching for identity beyond being that of a maidservant. Abraham was faithful, a true friend of God, someone who modeled the opposite of poverty in mission, and yet, as we said before, even he was capable of letting man's ways of mission sneak in briefly before re-establishing His walk of trust, joining the Lord once again in His best, non-watered-down plans.

. . . But imitate those who through faith and patience inherit the promises. (Hebrews 6:12)

Our poverty in mission usually stems from one of these ingredients having gone missing: *faith or patience.* For many of us, one or the other is a more natural strength, or one that we are more used to persevering in. However, it requires a lot of trust in God alone, far beyond self, man's ways or the world's measurements in order to live these two out together. I know a lot of people, even streams of the church or whole movements of mission that tend to function in one better than the other. Often, someone will have immense faith in God that He can do something, but little patience to wait for Him to establish it in His ways and timing. Other times, someone will have all the patience in the world to let go and surrender to God's ways and His will, but is unable to apply much faith towards God's ability to actually move powerfully and beyond human means. A big part of seeing our poverty healed is found in refusing to operate merely out of our personal God-given strength, and letting God strengthen the other side so that both faith and patience can co-labor together. When faith and patience co-labor together in our lives simultaneously, it empowers us to better co-labor with God.

One of the clearest ways to see our poverty in mission wiped away is to see these areas of faith and patience healed together. When we truly trust God, we have no reason to get ahead of Him in mission, which as we learned from Ishmael, can actually add conflict that will war against the true purposes and promises of God. When we trust God to perform what He has promised, we have no reason not to wait as long as it takes, knowing that His word never returns void (Isaiah 55:11) and that He will establish His own purpose, mission or promise far better than we ever could.

Moving Forward:

1. What did it mean for Abraham to "birth an Ishmael"?

2. Discuss the underrated power of trust. Describe why it is so important for us to learn to allow faith and patience to co-labor together in our lives of mission.

3. Have you ever birthed some form of an "Ishmael" by getting ahead of God, applying His promises through your means, or seeking worth and identity? What was it? Perhaps the promise was right, and God is ready for you to birth its "Isaac" form now. What might that look like?

Part 3: Living Identity

As we began to talk about in the Introduction, ministry and mission often keep us seeking to identify what it is we are "doing" to support the value of our mission, or our participation in such. I love *doing*, and *going*, but I am constantly challenged in each new season to see from God's perspective *who* He has created us to "be." This is the basic question of identity: Are we living *for* identity, or *from* identity? Our mission will change dramatically based on our answer.

Identity gets lost in mission, pretty naturally, to tell you the truth. Yet, we certainly can't reveal true identity in Christ to others if we ourselves are not walking in our own. We tend to try to measure up to what we perceive our lives in mission are *supposed* to look like rather than freely operating from the place of internal worth and true identity that God has purposed within us for mission. I consider this to be one of our greatest recovery missions—a recovery of the unique mission that is alive within you, which has value that stems not from ways of *doing* that are measured externally, but from *being* who God made you to be, living out your truest identity. To put it simply, what we *do* for Christ can't measure up to who we *are* in Christ. Or in other words, it's not until the *"Be"* and the *"Who"* overtake the *"What"* and the *"Do"* that God can be most productive through us. (I imagine that's how Dr. Seuss would have said it anyway.)

Our poverty in mission stems from this dilemma. If we don't know or accept who we are in and through God's eyes, we will always try to prove our identity through what we do, or accomplish. But when that kind of orphan heart within us is allowed to be filled up by the Father's seemingly too-good-to-be-true unconditional love, then we can see ourselves as He sees us, and live much more powerfully and effectively *from* that unique identity inside us instead of *for* a different identity that we try to find in the world around us.

The basis of our identity must come from God's love for us. It's about receiving. Often, in mission, we learn to subscribe to the much more "religious" stance of giving. And, giving is great, wonderful and absolutely necessary! But it can't happen without first receiving. Receiving is one of the most powerful things we can do in mission because it sets the table so that others can later come to eat as well. How often, though, do we struggle to receive God's love freely rather than trying to earn it? If we are holding on to that misconception of needing to earn His love in the slightest way, then it is going to leak out into what we pass on to others. Our own internal, spiritual poverty can actually increase another's physical poverty. We have to go back to the basics of receiving love. It's not enough to learn to see others as God sees them, because if we don't learn to see ourselves the way God sees us and to love ourselves the way God loves us, then we certainly won't be able to pass His best on to others.

Based on His love, we receive our identity first from Christ Himself, who is a living embodiment of the Father's love for us. But Jesus didn't just die to save us physically the way we might save an orphan from starvation; He did us one better than that. He rose again with new life and then ascended into heaven, from where He sent us His Holy Spirit, part of His promise that He will never leave us orphans. Our spiritual poverty has no basis in reality, no matter what lies the enemy tries to feed you. Jesus said it Himself, so make these words your own:

> *"Let not your heart be troubled; you believe in God, believe also in Me. In My Father's house are many mansions; if it were not so, I would have told you. I go to prepare a place for you. And if I go and prepare a place for you, I will come again and receive you to Myself; that where I am, there you may be also. . . . "*

> *"And I will pray the Father, and He will give you another Helper, that He may abide with you forever—the Spirit of truth, whom the world cannot receive, because it neither sees Him nor knows Him; but you know Him, for*

He dwells with you and will be in you. I will not leave you orphans; I will come to you." (John 14:1-3, 16-18)

We are not simply orphans who have been saved. We are not just saved servants, either. We have been made an actual part of the family. We have become "like Christ," as we often say, but it's not limited to our actions of service and love. It's also our new nature. By Jesus' death on the cross and His resurrection, we have been made sons and daughters of God. His Spirit bears witness of such. Our identity is not that of a saved orphan still trying to prove our worth or beg for a spot at the table—our identity is nothing less than sons and daughters of our heavenly Father, with full access to the table.

For as many as are led by the Spirit of God, these are sons of God. For you did not receive the spirit of bondage again to fear, but you received the Spirit of adoption by whom we cry out, "Abba, Father." The Spirit Himself bears witness with our spirit that we are children of God. (Romans 8:14-16)

Did you hear that? We are no longer left prey to our fears and insecurities, which means we don't have to try to prove ourselves or cover those areas by what we do. That works-oriented bondage has been taken away. We have already been proven worthy in Christ, we have been filled by the Spirit, and we must live and give from *that* place instead of from our works. Simply put, our identity in Christ has more to give than our hands do.

As believers, by the deposit of the Spirit within us, we are all sons and daughters. But also, each of us is created to be different on purpose, and such differences should help us establish the unique harvest field God has called us to, whether that is in the church, the marketplace, arts, media, sports, government or any other form of mission locally or abroad. I believe that in order for us to have a powerful "what" to do in mission, each of us must know our own special alignment with God and the unique identity of "who" we are created to be. You will then be free from trying to measure up to others or to the world's ways, free from comparing, free from compromising the unique differences of mission within you that the Father calls His own. He is going to use you to reach people no one else will reach, with gifts no one else has, in places others won't go. Your life, and therefore your mission, is *supposed* to look different. Theodore Roosevelt once said, "Comparison is the thief of joy." Wow, did he nail it! I can't even count the number of times I've robbed myself—*and especially God*—of joy simply because I started comparing and measuring myself against others, instead of simply shining out of the confidence of who He has made me to be. Some of the very differences in your life that you may be insecure about are actually unique craftsmanship by the Father through which He plans to impact others. Be who He has made you to be, and your true purpose and mission will certainly flow from there.

Many books could be written on the subject of identity alone, but for now, our identity stems from these two unique truths: 1. We are children of God, not orphans. We have nothing more to prove. He loves us as His own and we must operate from our security in His complete love. 2. You are unique, and amazingly different in persona, purpose, gifting and calling—*and God digs that about you!* So, don't ever stop being you. And if you haven't started, now is a great time to begin. It will literally change the way you do mission, as you will give out of God's storehouse instead of your own.

Moving Forward:

1. What is your true identity in Christ? What could that mean

to mission if you were to live it out?

2. Describe the difference between doing mission *for* identity vs. living mission *from* identity. What does it mean to say: "Our identity in Christ has more to give than our hands do"?

3. How does comparison become the thief of joy? How does this impact mission?

Part 4: Jacob & Us

What happens when we leave our poverty in mission behind? We are free to stop searching for the approval of man, and we get to dream with God. We see this clearly lived out by Jacob after he received the "Father's Blessing" discussed earlier. Abraham gave the blessing to Isaac, and Isaac imparted it to Jacob. The blessing released Jacob from a life of striving. We are often blinded by our focus on man's approval, missing out the whole time on what the Father is ready to do, and what we're called to join Him in. He is waiting to bless us, to use us and to multiply through us. However, it's hard to receive God's blessing when we are still looking for man's blessing. It's hard to see what *God* is doing when we're looking so wholeheartedly for people's reaction to what *we* are doing. Jacob was no different until he received that special blessing that ended his prior search, setting his life on a new track and, eventually, a new mission. Jacob's life after the blessing was Jacob's new life after being freed from spiritual poverty. It was the beginning of his learning, however gradually, to dream greater dreams *with* God.

Jacob's life after the blessing sets the stage for a series of events in which God's momentum in his life began to grow and build, until it eventually burst into multiplication! Jacob was about to leave home and blaze his own trail, leaving behind the strife with Esau that had followed them from birth, culminating in Esau's trading his birthright for a bowl of stew, and Jacob's plotting to receive the blessing. Their strife is still alive today, as is the strife between poverty and purpose. Like Esau, we often trade in one for the other, long-term purpose for short-term feelings of self-worth and survival—even when our heart cries for something more. Jacob had to get beyond this strife, and so must we. We can't live lives of purpose while that impoverished spirit still lives within us; battling insecurities, keeping measurements, and striving for worldly self-worth. The two war against one another. Jacob received the blessing, found new, albeit still unknown identity and purpose, and had to begin to venture into the new life God had set out before him. It would be a long journey, but the blessing paved the way for transformation to begin. Before Jacob left, Isaac blessed him once more with the blessing of his father, Abraham.

"May God Almighty bless you, and make you fruitful and multiply you, that you may be an assembly of peoples; and give you the blessing of Abraham, to you and your descendants with you, that you may inherit the land in which you are a stranger, which God gave to Abraham." (Genesis 28:3-4)

After the blessing, Jacob moved forward into greater purpose, and new mission, though it still took time for him to fully embrace that mission. His mission wouldn't be self-oriented anymore, nor would his mission merely possess fruit—but the fruit would forever multiply. The same becomes true for us when we start to leave behind old ways and mindsets. We are able to move beyond the spiritual poverty that is like a hidden leak inside us, once it gets sealed by the blood of Jesus. We, too, can then move into a new life and form of mission that doesn't attempt to mix our water with God's oil anymore. We can start a new journey where hidden self needs and motives are removed from our mission so we can begin to take on His nature and live from the identity He has given us; a journey in which we begin to bring His promises to life, eventually multiplying with Him in the ways He is moving. We're no longer trying to get filled from filling others; now we are free to give from a Source that never needs refilling, because we know to Whom we belong. Our identity is designed to birth a God-sized mission of its own, if we'll allow it to come forth. Jacob's journey took time, but the blessing set his course to find true purpose, and then discover his God-given identity that eventually shaped the mission and impact of his life, not just for short-term fruit, but long-term multiplication.

Specifically, Jacob's blessing paved a path to Bethel, a famous encounter that we now familiarly refer to as Jacob's ladder. I wonder if we would know of that encounter between Jacob and God if not for the blessing from Isaac that started Jacob's course forward? Whether he knew it consciously or not at this point, Jacob now lived with a new freedom as the blessing of man had been fulfilled in his life. He didn't need to search for his identity or purpose anymore, or remain blind to what could be received directly from the Father. Isaac had given Jacob a "father's blessing," which gave powerful release; but at Bethel, through what we now know as the story of Jacob's ladder, God began to give Jacob a *"Father's Blessing"* that redefined his foundation and the possibilities of mission through his life. This encounter would multiply for generations, and shake whole nations!

So he came to a certain place and stayed there all night, because the sun had set. And he took one of the stones of that place and put it at his head, and he lay down in that place to sleep. Then he dreamed, and behold, a ladder was set up on the earth, and its top reached to heaven, and there the angels of God were ascending and descending on it. And behold, the Lord stood above it and said: "I am the Lord God of Abraham your father and the God of Isaac; the land on which you lie I will give to you and your descendants. Also, your descendants shall be as the dust of the earth; you shall spread abroad to the west and the east, to the north and the south; and in you and in your seed all the families of the earth shall be blessed. Behold, I am with you and will keep you wherever you go, and will bring you back to this land; for I will not leave you until I have done what I have spoken to you."

Then Jacob awoke from his sleep and said, "Surely the Lord is in this place, and I did not know it." And he was afraid and said, "How awesome is this place! This is none other than the house of God, and this is the gate of heaven!" (Genesis 28:11-17)

Do you see what God did there? He used Isaac's blessing and took it to a whole new level! God expanded man's mission and purpose—*man's blessing*—so man could join Him in *His* mission and purpose. That's what God wants to do for all of us in the missions and purposes He has for our lives. The first blessing sets the stage for the second one. But so many of us, without ever having been given that first unconditional blessing from man, never allow ourselves to receive the second one straight from God. We find ourselves too busy searching to fill that internal poverty, never able to rest and realize what God wants to impart to us straight from His Father's heart. Imagine what God has in store for your life as you join Him and allow those areas of insecurity, desire for belonging, and spiritual poverty to truly be filled up once and for all. Imagine when our mission, currently mixed with a fruitless search for self-worth and identity, is purified by the Father so that we receive our own version of Jacob's ladder and can start a new course of mission fulfilled in Him. There will be exponential growth in our lives, through our lives, and in the spread of His kingdom here on earth as it is in heaven.

As we have discussed, when we don't live under the premise of the "Father's Blessing" of unconditional love and approval, fully aware of God's special vision for our lives, we tend to live from a place of proving and striving. Also, we start to expect the same from others. There is no rest in that. But look where Jacob's ladder finds its foundation: ***"And he took one of the stones of that place and put it at his head, and he lay down in that place to sleep."*** Huh? Are you kidding? Jacob was so at rest, finally free from strife, that even a stone pillow could become a place of rest where he could *begin* to dream with God. This place of rest from our striving for significance is vital to our life and calling in mission. This place of peace, secure in our identity in Christ, is where He can give us our own vision, straight from Him, for the mission He has created us to join Him in. That is where true purpose in our life begins!

Look at something else Jacob said just after his encounter with God: ***"Surely the Lord is in this place, and I did not know it."*** How profound! Jacob realized that God had already been there, more present than he knew, waiting for Jacob to receive something new so that He could empower Jacob forward into *His* best purposes for Jacob's life. Could that same statement be true for you? Not just in mission, but in life? Is there a chance that we have been living life and doing mission through our own eyes, with much striving, perhaps from that place of internal poverty that we couldn't even recognize? What if you suddenly realized that all this time you had been blinded to the greater realities of God, His love and the mission and purpose that are already present and waiting? What if your eyes only need to awaken out of their slumber of insecurity to see through Love's expectation that His life and mission are already at hand? That's what God did for Jacob at Bethel. That's what God is awakening in us!

At Bethel, God began to show and impart to Jacob new purpose. It took Jacob time to step into this purpose, but the journey had begun and God would see it through. Eventually, He did. We read of another encounter between God and Jacob in which Jacob received a new identity—an identity that would bring forth all the purpose and mission that had been promised through Jacob's life but that he had been wrestling with all the while.

> *Then Jacob was left alone; and a Man wrestled with him until the breaking of day. Now when He saw that He did not prevail against him, He touched the socket of his hip; and the socket of Jacob's hip was out of joint as He wrestled with him. And He said, "Let Me go, for the day breaks." But he said, "I will not let You go unless You bless me!"*
>
> *So He said to him, "What is your name?" He said, "Jacob." And He said, "Your name shall no longer be called Jacob, but Israel; for you have struggled with God and with men, and have prevailed." (Genesis 32:24-28)*

Jacob's wrestling with God in this passage is such an accurate metaphor of his, and our own, wrestling with identity in life and mission. Jacob stepped forward and allowed his faith to begin to take hold of what had already been given to him. The blessing illuminated the life God had placed before Jacob and helped increase his ability to embrace the change that was possible and the plans God was preparing ahead. It gave Jacob new vision for what he was wrestling for. And by the time he had prevailed in the battle, Jacob had been given a new name—a new identity! Anything was possible now, for Jacob saw with new eyes that weren't searching for mankind's approval, eyes that found rest from strife, eyes that were free to see what God wanted him to see, and to be who God created him to be.

God wants to, and actually already has, given us a new foundation to operate from. Many of us wrestle for an identity that He has already freely given us. Jacob wrestled with his true identity for more years than this passage shows. He had an incredible purpose that both Isaac and his heavenly Father had laid out for him. But it wasn't until he was victorious in his wrestling and received his new identity that such powerful mission and multiplication to the nations and generations could come forth through his life. Are you still wrestling and striving for a purpose or identity that God has already given you? Are you searching for something on the outside that God has already blessed you with on the inside? Perhaps there is more purpose and mission present in your life than you know, more than you could ever "do" in many lifetimes. Perhaps the only thing keeping these purposes from coming about is the fact that you haven't yet received the new identity of love, belonging, value and purpose that the Father already sees you in.

God, your Father and my Father, has a "Father's Blessing" for you that has no substitutes. He wants to give you your own "Jacob's ladder" testimony, complete with fresh vision for your life, containing the mission and purpose *He* has created you for. He wants to be your Source. He waits to press His heart into yours and help you see through His eyes. He wants you to know your true identity in Him, and He wants you to understand that it is not something you have to strive or wrestle for. It is an identity within

His family that you multiply *from*, enlarging His family legacy through your own place of belonging. You are a child of God like no other. You are of value to Him simply because you are *you*. That value is not conditional on service, but on the identity you have in Christ. Mission doesn't lead you *to* your identity; mission begins *from* your identity. God is waiting for you there to journey forward with you in ways you could never dream of on your own. So, dream with the Father! You are loved. His love for you is unconditional, perfect, without blemish or loophole. His love for you is big enough to feed the nations, but He wants you to feast on His love first, for that is how His bread and fishes multiply—through His love *in you!*

He has created you with purpose that no one else has. You are beautifully, and wonderfully, unique. The premise of comparison is among the greatest of lies because it implies that there is someone or something you are supposed to measure up to. "One of a kind" is not just a cultural saying; it is a divine truth that we've allowed familiarity to weaken. God put a unique piece of His heart in you that will make a difference in the world, so don't try to change that part of you—*it has purpose!* God put it there to shine differently from anyone else, and it pleases Him. Go and mine deeply with God for His purpose within you, and then freely dream it out with Him! The Father loves to dream with you.

And finally, you must always remember just how much God believes in you. There are also many more all around you who may not always know how to say it, but they believe in you, too. Don't let the enemy sneak his lies into moments or places of silence, but let those places instead be filled with daily reminders of the Father's blessing over you and His belief in you. He gave you your unique purpose because He believed that there was no one better in the world to carry such purpose and mission out to the world. That is the mission to grab hold of—*with Him!* He believes in you so much that He will both plow and dance with you every step of the way, in the dry places and in the moments of joy!

Go! Find your own Bethel with God. Wait on Him with expectation, knowing that surely God is already in that place and you didn't even know it. Your Bethel will be a place where that internal, spiritual poverty will be replaced by a new sense of identity in Him and your new counter-cultural mission will begin. God believes in you, and so must you. He can already see your new life! Don't continue wrestling! Freely accept the identity the Father has already given you—live and give from that place right now.

Moving Forward:

1. What is the difference between man's blessing and the Father's? What is the difference in allowing Him to be your Source?

2. How does the Father want you to dream with Him? How might this impact the mission and purpose that flows from your life?

3. Describe in your own words the Father's Blessing that He speaks over you and the identity He's given you to live and do mission from.

End Notes:

1. Eugene H. Peterson, *The Message: The Bible in Contemporary Language* (Colorado Springs, CO: NavPress, 2002).
2. Jeff Silbar, Larry Henley, "The Wind Beneath My Wings" [Bette Midler], copyright © 1988 by Atlantic – PR2615-2, audio CD.

CHAPTER 6:

"THEIR" POVERTY IN MISSION

Part 1: "Berhanu's" Story

When I first met "Berhanu" (name changed for privacy) I was overcome with heartache and compassion for his outer condition. In fact, I was so focused upon his outer condition that I could have easily missed what God wanted to do inside him. He lived on the streets and was just about to turn fourteen. A lot of kids on the streets have many things in common, but Berhanu faced a challenge few others ever had; he had no arms.

Berhanu's arms had been lost in an accident while he was playing near a railroad track some three years earlier. He had stumps at his shoulders, but a smile that could light up a room. Berhanu started meeting up with the other kids and our team of spiritual fathers and mothers on a regular basis. The first time I met him was at one of our "street church" gatherings. My heart sank as I saw his sleeves drooping down, but my spirits were lifted when I saw the way the other kids interacted with him, especially how they served him so selflessly. I will never forget watching another boy patiently feed Berhanu his breakfast. One bite at a time, the boy tore off a piece of bread and dipped it into the tea, helping him to enjoy both at once. Berhanu sat receiving his breakfast with immense humility and grace, though I had to wonder how this made him feel deep inside—was it a struggle for him to hide his hurt and shame?

One of the ways we empowered the kids on the street was to purchase goods for them to sell, usually a tray full of cookies, tissues, gum and the like. The other most common option was to buy them a shoeshine box. This empowered them to work, and we coupled this with getting them re-started in a local school. Berhanu obviously was less likely to shine shoes—though we did find out he was very adept at utilizing his feet for hands—so we set him up with a tray of goods to sell. As you can imagine, two things happened for Berhanu. One, some people would go above and beyond in their generosity towards him because of his disability, by paying him a little extra tip, or showing him some other kindness to help out. The second sort of encounter Berhanu would run into, though, wasn't so friendly: other kids on the street cycling in their own poverty, just waiting to take advantage of him. Not only would they lift the tray that was hung around his neck straight off him for themselves, but they'd also reach into his pockets and steal all his profits, knowing there wasn't a thing about it he could do. This occurrence didn't need to happen much for us to realize that something had to be done.

We were in the middle of setting up the first street shelter where the boys would live, but it was still going to take a few more weeks before it was ready. We paid for the other kids to stay each night in a local shelter, but this wouldn't work anymore for Berhanu. He needed a different answer, an answer God now asked us to provide.

Like many of the kids on the streets, Berhanu did have a family living in the countryside. Also, like many of the other kids, the extreme poverty they lived in caused huge rifts in the home, stirring up various forms of abuse, irrational fights, lack of food or opportunity, and a greatly impoverished hope. This lack of hope is why most of the kids leave home, actually, even the ones who still have a good family—they go into the city searching for a glimmer of hope. Berhanu had a father and mother at home who loved him, and several siblings as well. But he battled all those things that many of the other kids battled, with one huge extra: His lack of arms brought on even greater discouragement and depression, not to mention bullying from the other kids in his village. He wanted nothing—and I mean *nothing*—to do with going home. He didn't want to make a phone call, or even talk about his family. It was a gaping wound that left a huge hole in his life, more so even than his arms.

We knew that until the street shelter was ready, and because he was unwilling to go back to his family, we needed to welcome Berhanu to live with us. Mind you, this wasn't any kind of a rash emotional decision, nor were we trying to be heroes. It was simple obedience. We had only a short time to decide, needing to remove him from the extra vulnerability he was experiencing on the streets. But we also needed to pray. We had to make sure that it was God's idea and not just ours. This was not a decision to be taken lightly. We had four daughters at home and were looking at welcoming in a fourteen-year-old boy from the streets. It was a very serious situation. God was gracious to give us several confirmations and wisdom regarding how to set up our home and his time with us. We also met with the other street kids first to explain the situation, not wanting any of them to feel left out or that Berhanu was being given preference. We wanted them to understand the circumstances he was battling. Truth be told, they knew his battles far better than we did. They were very gracious and understanding—at least the majority of them—and wanted what was best for Berhanu. It was a proud moment seeing their responses of love towards him, even though they knew they weren't the ones coming to live with us.

So we invited Berhanu to our home, letting him know he would be considered part of the family and could stay with us until the shelter was ready for him. Needless to say, he was thrilled to take us up on our offer and arrived swiftly to join us. We began to learn a lot about Berhanu, which was easy because he spoke

English well compared to most of the kids. His English proficiency stemmed from one of those surprising nuggets he let us in on. See, Berhanu may have only been fourteen, and he may have been living on the streets, but he had also been to America. Yes, you read that right. *Berhanu had been to America!* We were shocked, too! He began to tell us all about it and then even went so far as to show us evidence of his time in the U.S., the family he had lived with for months, and the goal of his visit, which was to receive a prosthetic arm—a very expensive, technologically built arm.

Obviously we weren't the first to meet Berhanu and take notice. But what dropped our jaws—and our hearts—even more was the fact that afterwards he was right back out on the streets. The family, the doctors and so many others who had loved him so well had no idea, either. As far as they knew, Berhanu had returned to a great family situation. He should have been flourishing with his new technological limb after having been given the gift of a lifetime. Unfortunately, that's not what happened, and there was no way for this generous family, who obviously loved him so much, to know that Berhanu had returned immediately to his old cycle of poverty. All the while, his new prosthetic arm sat at his family's home unused, worth more than his family would typically earn over years and years combined. This realization left us heartbroken, seeing the grip that poverty has on the inside, even while external needs are generously and extravagantly fulfilled.

I don't share this at all to indict the family who supplied this gift to Berhanu. Their intentions and giving were through the roof. His story is simply a sad portrayal of the secret life of poverty and how it slithers about to keep its grip on lives from the inside, waiting for us to feed it further. We were still intending to love Berhanu in a way similar to that of the previous family, largely focused on addressing his outer poverty. We were praying for new arms for him, too! And when I say this, I understand that many people have a different take on miracles and whether they still occur today. Though this is neither the topic nor the focus of this book, I will share plainly that I believe that miracles do still occur today. I have been an active recipient and participant too many times not to believe. I've watched Biblical-sized miracles happen before our eyes; I've seen growths disappear and a foot healed, and we know many others who have witnessed far more. I had known of stories from great friends who have witnessed missing limbs such as Berhanu's being re-grown. Believing this way, why would we not begin asking the Father for new arms for Berhanu? Sure, it might sound a little crazy, but the least we could do is ask, *and believe*. Our Father is good like that; He left His Spirit to operate through us in these ways and often waits for us to join Him in such prayers. But the purpose of this story is not to convince you of miracles. I simply want you to understand where we were initially coming from in addressing Berhanu's poverty and lack. There are many different ways in which we good-heartedly address external needs. Just as his first family from America had, we focused on his outward circumstances and hoped to see some form of healing. This is a common theme in mission, to start on the outside and work our way in, whether through healing, medical attention, resources or meeting other physical needs. I am not trying to discount these necessities, but once again, in mission, and especially with regard to poverty, we are called to recognize that God sees differently than we do. The simple fact that Berhanu had his needs met with such abundance and yet still ended up away from his family and back on the streets without his new arm reminds us that there is a deeper level of poverty God wants to address through us—the healing of hearts.

As we prayed for Berhanu's arms to be restored, as well as for other needs in his life to be met, the Lord reminded me of the compassion that often preceded Jesus' miracles (see Chapter 3). However, I knew this isn't a superficial kind of compassion that is "feelings" or "emotions" oriented. It's the kind of compassion that can bear a burden from a deep core of understanding what someone else is going through. It was then, in response to those prayers asking the Lord to teach me such compassion for Berhanu, that God put a challenge before me: *"How can you know what Berhanu truly goes through if you have not experienced such yourself?"* And you know what? He was right. Imagine that! I had seen but didn't fully know the kind of suffering Berhanu battled each day, but I was committed to understanding. It was clear what I had to do. I would live for twenty-four hours without using my arms, having them bandaged to my body so I couldn't cheat even once.

God wanted me to experience deeper roots of understanding when it came to the poverty we were battling in anyone's life, not just Berhanu's. "Their" poverty in mission releases a deep heart cry, a cry that comes from beyond their struggles to eat, walk or overcome other outward limitations. Their heart cry is to break out of the cycles that poverty is birthed from and has trapped them in. Their poverty isn't simply a place of lack or overwhelming needs. If only these needs are met then they will merely have vision for living up to those earthly standards of fulfillment. God, their Father, has greater vision and purpose for their lives. And each heart in poverty usually has a deep heart wound that needs to be healed, sealed and built upon as a new foundation. Berhanu was teaching this to us at a new level, and I was about to learn firsthand.

Moving Forward:

1. Why do you think we so quickly and naturally focus upon meeting external needs, working from the outside in rather than from the inside out?

2. Can you remember and describe a time in which you naturally reacted to external needs or poverty rather than stepping back to inquire of God and see with His eyes?

3. What does the fact that Berhanu had been so abundantly provided for yet still ended up back on the streets tell you about poverty's true root?

Part 2: A New Heart Goes Further

Let me start out by saying that my plan of "going without arms for a day" wasn't as simple as it may sound. I have had several broken arms and serious shoulder injuries that required my arm to be immobilized and pressed against my chest for weeks. Even one day of this was *completely* different! We rely on our arms and their natural presence far more than we realize for things such as balance and other functions we may take for granted. Also, before I could go through with my plan there were two people I had to bring in on the decision: First, I needed to ask my wife's permission, because, as you can probably imagine, there would be *a lot* I would need her help for—*a lot!* Once Destiny had graciously given approval to her vital part in this (her part may even have been harder than mine), then I needed to share with Berhanu some of what was going on in our hearts. We wanted to honor him in every bit of this, not just from our perspective, but from his as well. We didn't focus on the "new arms" we were praying for as much as we let him know that we believed God wanted to do a greater work in his life, and we wanted to join in. I made it very clear that this was not funny to me; it was not a joke, but something I took very seriously because of his value to us, and to God. Berhanu was very receptive, smiled about it, and, truth be told, couldn't wait for me to begin. I think he was genuinely blessed and looked forward to someone understanding even one percent of the reality of his life. We finished the planning, and made sure that my twenty-four hour span would include a busy day full of responsibilities for me. If I were to be just sitting around the house, I'd only get a measure of what I could learn. It had to happen on one of my peak days.

I decided to start the clock at about 10 pm, knowing I'd have to go through one night of sleep in total. For me, that sleep was one of the most challenging parts of the whole twenty-four hours. I was miserably uncomfortable all night, having forgotten just how much I move and position my arms even at night for comfort. To have them strapped down felt torturous—*and that was just while sleeping!*

I won't go through the whole twenty-four hours with you, but let's just say there were a lot of challenges in what we consider menial day-to-day activities, things we take for granted; like eating, showering, or going to the bathroom. It was extremely difficult to be forced to constantly receive help in these humbling ways. Also, I was used to being driven with ideas, hopes, vision and purpose. But now, suddenly, my opportunities felt limited. My situation discouraged my hope much more quickly than I anticipated. There was less I could dream to do, and little I could start or finish on my own. I didn't know where to begin. That's when I really started to understand Berhanu's poverty—not just understanding him through knowledge with my mind—but with my heart. I felt his plight, and the places where identity took a beating. I felt the tiniest touch of the pounding his heart must take from things like shame and hopelessness. It is discouraging to continually be dependent on someone else, even for the tiniest of life's minute details. There is a lot of discontent, and the poisons of hope deferred try to inject themselves quickly when you feel so restricted in dreams and possibilities. I mean, I couldn't even go to the bathroom by myself, let alone figure out some of the more purposeful things I wanted to get started on.

These limitations may seem easy to overcome, but they can be crushing to a heart and force someone into deeper levels of poverty than *our* eyes ever see. That's when it hit me. The Lord had given me exactly what I had asked for through this twenty-four hours without arms. He showed me Berhanu's healing. Berhanu didn't need new arms as much as he first needed a new heart! God could give him new arms any day of the week, but He was a Father broken over the internal and unseen wounds of his young son, looking for someone who would embrace the mission field that consisted of the cracks and bruises of his heart. We could now see what we were only partially aware of before. This kind of heart healing goes beyond someone repeating a prayer of external words for salvation (which Berhanu had already done), and truly allows the Lord's love to come in and speak life over what poverty and hope deferred had tried to destroy.

I took this back to the Lord in prayer to ask for His strategy: *"Father, how do You want to give Berhanu a new heart?"* He led me to a passage in the book of Ezekiel that I still hold onto for strategy today:

> *"I will give you a new heart and put a new spirit within you; I will take the heart of stone out of your flesh and give you a heart of flesh. I will put My Spirit within you and cause you to walk in My statutes, and you will keep My judgments and do them. Then you shall dwell in the land that I gave to your fathers; you shall be My people, and I will be your God.*
>
> *"I will deliver you from all your uncleannesses. I will call for the grain and multiply it, and bring no famine upon you. And I will multiply the fruit of your trees and the increase of your fields, so that you need never again bear the reproach of famine among the nations. . . ."*
>
> *'Thus says the Lord God: "On the day that I cleanse you from all your iniquities, I will also enable you to dwell in the cities, and the ruins shall be rebuilt. The desolate land shall be tilled instead of lying desolate in the sight of all who pass by. So they will say, 'This land that was desolate has become like the garden of Eden; and the wasted, desolate, and ruined cities are now fortified and inhabited.' Then the nations which are left all around you shall know that I, the Lord, have rebuilt the ruined places and planted what was desolate. I, the Lord, have spoken it, and I will do it." (Ezekiel 36: 26-30, 33-36)*

What a conclusion to the passage! *"I will do it,"* says the Lord. And with Berhanu, *He* certainly did. It wasn't our ways of mission that brought transformation to Berhanu's life; it was God's supernatural gift of a new heart. To me, this passage became such an inspiring picture of multiplication. Multiplication starts with the one, the one heart being healed of true poverty. This brings a new spirit, cleaned of the old wounds that plagued it as the engine behind poverty's cycle and free to transform from that new heart into a land that is no longer desolate, but so fruitful it becomes once again like the Garden of Eden. This is what I believe now for every life we address in poverty; each in its own unique way. We saw it happen firsthand in and through Berhanu, who taught us so much about *"their"* poverty.

With Berhanu, we took this passage literally, believing that God wanted to bring it to life in his heart. I went to a number of our local team members and to our family and shared further what the Lord had shared with me. We thought we needed to have a time of prayer over Berhanu and lay hands on him together, showering him with love and praying for God's new heart in his life to replace the wounded one poverty had bludgeoned. I asked Berhanu if he would be open to receiving this ministry. He agreed, and we all gathered together one afternoon in our living room to believe God for Berhanu's new heart. It was a powerful time of prayer. God's presence and love were palpable, and though we couldn't see any physical changes with our eyes, we knew the Father had gone to work in Berhanu's heart.

The next day Berhanu came to me and asked if it would be okay for him to call his parents. I was completely surprised and almost didn't know what to say. I actually questioned him because of the sheer amount of stubbornness he had always shown in everything relating to his home and family. But now he was coming to us, the very day after God had set us on *His* mission towards Berhanu's truest poverty. He called home and had a very good conversation with his mom. The next day Berhanu came to us yet again with a new request that almost worried us at first: *"I'm ready to go home to my family. Can you take me home now?"* Whoa! Again, we questioned him to make sure he was ready, trying to figure out how he could change from one strong opinion to the polar opposite so rapidly. Was he truly prepared for such a drastic change already? We didn't want him to rush into it and cause more problems again. But Berhanu was certain in his stance, and we were not about to stand in the way of what God was doing. It was such a vivid portrayal of part of that Ezekiel 36 passage: *"On the day that I cleanse you from all your iniquities, I will also enable you to dwell in the cities, and the ruins shall be rebuilt."* God had done this for Berhanu just as He said He would. Rome may not be built in a day, but God can heal any heart of even great depths of poverty in but one short day.

Berhanu returned home accompanied by a couple members of our team of spiritual fathers and mothers. They built a relationship with his family the same way we built one with Berhanu. The team would not only visit with Berhanu like they once did on the streets, but now, they were also visiting his whole family with the same love and care. Now *that* is multiplication! God took the heart He healed in Berhanu and began to spread that same healing to his whole family. Before we knew it, Berhanu's family was able to move into a new home, started taking new steps forward in life, and even began reaching out to other distant family members in other parts of the country. Berhanu's new heart, just as the passage laid out, led to a desolate land being made fruitful again. And for the remaining years of his adolescence, Berhanu never ran away from home again. For the first time, the restlessness of his pain and lack of hope didn't drive him away. God healed Berhanu's poverty through a mission different than where we had begun, and different from where mission usually begins.

When we begin to address "their" poverty in mission, we must begin in the same place God wants to heal in us, from the inside out. Poverty is not relegated to cycles of dirty, torn clothes or empty bellies. Poverty is first a condition of the heart, which, in everyone, needs to be restored and made new. Berhanu never even made it to our mission's street shelter because God had already done something deeper, entirely eliminating his external need. "Their" poverty won't be eradicated until we let go and listen to the internal need God first wants us to *join Him* in addressing. We can give someone a meal, or even a new arm. Both of those are amazing and often essential gifts of love and care, giving that we should not abandon. However, even those gifts will get lost in the draining whirlpool of poverty if the heart is not first healed. Then once the heart is healed, those gifts not only can remain, but they can multiply further than anything we can hope or imagine.

Moving Forward:

1. Describe the inner battles of poverty that Berhanu's heart had been bludgeoned with. How do you think these same battles uncontrollably plague others you reach out to on the mission field in unseen ways?

2. Discuss the cycle of new life in the passage from Ezekiel 36 that helps not only break but reverse the cycle of poverty.

3. How can you apply this "new heart story" to your own life, mission and hopes of seeing poverty destroyed?

Part 3: Purpose Over Poverty

This section stems directly from the discussion regarding our own poverty in mission and its counterpart in discovering our true identity. We often use the word poverty as though it were the identity of someone fighting off its grip. But poverty is no more a person's identity than would be another outward limitation or shortcoming, such as a disability or physical trait. Referring to such things would usually be considered an insult, and they certainly do not define one's identity. Neither is poverty an identity. As discussed before, we are part of a great transformation that must take place in the transition from an identity founded in poverty to one founded in God. We are part of a season of mission that calls for a revival of true identity. Until we see our own internal poverty eliminated, we can't fully help others to discover their true identity. But when you do begin to walk in this new nature and renewed mindset of your own, you will be amazed at the power you carry to reproduce such in others.

As we talked about regarding "Berhanu," no matter what he received physically, it all kept going down a black hole until that internal lack was healed. While working with the kids from the street in Ethiopia we often passed along a number of my hand-me-down items of clothing for them to wear. However, these gifts didn't raise their status in society and cause them to act like someone no longer walking in poverty. Rather, we often saw them only one week later, the clothing already tattered and filthy, our gift of something new swept up into their old cycles rather than the other way around. Our benevolence in mission will continue to be swept into these old cycles until we reproduce something new, something different—something that cannot be given by mere hands but which passes on from one healed heart to another.

When we begin walking in our own identity in Christ as sons and daughters, we will reproduce the very same. The end to others' poverty starts with us. We must live out that which their hearts long to receive. Our new foundation in mission will give them a new foundation in life. Thus, the heart posture of living from one's true identity among the broken around the world remains one of our most uncharted of mission opportunities. Let's look back at one of the passages we emphasized regarding our own poverty in mission.

For as many as are led by the Spirit of God, these are sons of God. For you did not receive the spirit of bondage again to fear, but you received the Spirit of adoption by whom we cry out, "Abba, Father." (Romans 8:14-15)

This verse has real meaning for us when discussing "their" poverty in mission. Every week during our largest "street church" gathering with the kids, immediately after breakfast we always began by declaring this verse out loud together in their language of Amharic. We wanted the kids to learn very early on in their new beliefs that they were not merely saved from hell, but they were already valued children of God! We often lead people only to that proverbial line to be crossed and rejoice that they made it there, but no matter how new a believer, I believe they need to be immediately shown the full foundation they've been given so they don't revert to a works-centered gospel on their way to becoming sons and daughters, nor allow old, familiar cycles back into their new life. There is a huge difference between receiving new life, and actually living new life—identity is key.

By declaring the passage from Romans 8 out loud so frequently, not only at these gatherings but almost daily as we met in smaller settings, the kids practiced their new identity in Christ; they spoke it out so consistently that it became a new pattern to replace their old patterns of poverty. The kids may have still looked impoverished in physical appearance, but there was little poverty left inside them. Unfortunately, in our typical approach we clean up the outside, pray for salvation on the inside, and then slowly work on their identity. I believe we have it backwards.

There is so much more that God has offered! See how Jesus handled this instance with Lazarus:

> **Jesus said, *"Take away the stone." Martha, the sister of him who was dead, said to Him, "Lord, by this time there is a stench, for he has been dead four days." Jesus said to her, "Did I not say to you that if you would believe you would see the glory of God?"***
>
> ***. . . He cried with a loud voice, "Lazarus, come forth!" And he who had died came out bound hand and foot with graveclothes, and his face was wrapped with a cloth. Jesus said to them, "Loose him, and let him go." (John 11: 39-40, 43-44)***

Jesus didn't focus first on dealing with the externals of graveclothes, stench, or what could have been considered unclean according to the law at the time. Instead, Jesus focused on the new life He was calling Lazarus into, and the rest became mere details to be taken care of after. I believe the same to be true as we work with others in poverty. We must call forth life according to the identity God sees them in, not minister to them according to the identity by which the world labels them. Again, poverty is not an identity to be walked out of—it was never an identity in the first place! We place too much focus on the graveclothes and the stench that can surround those the enemy has robbed. God calls to them the way Jesus called to Lazarus, asking us to move the stone while calling forth new life—sons and daughters.

Of course this doesn't mean we don't take care of the externals, too, because poverty is a very real battle. But it's a battle much more easily fought once we have dealt with its foundations of life and identity—then we can work our way back out to the things we plainly see. The unseen root is what feeds the more apparent needs of the fruit. When we call forth their identity as a son or daughter in Christ, showing them they already belong to a large, flourishing family and an even bigger Father, we give people new authority with which to overcome their own poverty. Otherwise, they are fighting a battle without any weapons, or without even knowing who the enemy is. That's a confusing and confounding battle for people to fight—no wonder it is such a challenge in mission. I long for the day identity in mission is valued the way the Father sees it. For then, we will see those who have been relegated to poverty arise with great kingdom purpose themselves and surprise us, and I hope even surpass us. Their purpose is greater than their poverty, their heart more valuable than their physical condition, and they wait to be transformed from empty vessels into vessels that carry a miraculous, multiplying oil, similar to what we read of in the following story.

A certain woman of the wives of the sons of the prophets cried out to Elisha, saying, "Your servant my husband is dead, and you know that your servant feared the Lord. And the creditor is coming to take my two sons to be his slaves."

So Elisha said to her, "What shall I do for you? Tell me, what do you have in the house?" And she said, "Your maidservant has nothing in the house but a jar of oil." Then he said, "Go, borrow vessels from everywhere, from all your neighbors—empty vessels; do not gather just a few. And when you have come in, you shall shut the door behind you and your sons; then pour it into all those vessels, and set aside the full ones."

So she went from him and shut the door behind her and her sons, who brought the vessels to her; and she poured it out. Now it came to pass, when the vessels were full, that she said to her son, "Bring me another vessel." And he said to her, "There is not another vessel." So the oil ceased. Then she came and told the man of God. And he said, "Go, sell the oil and pay your debt; and you and your sons live on the rest." (2 Kings 4:1-7)

This is quite the case of a family battling poverty. The widow was so indebted that she was about to lose her two sons. And what was it that God chose to use to miraculously multiply the oil? *Empty vessels*. Few of us would see the worth in an empty vessel, especially when we need to accumulate value for something so urgent. But here is that battle of internal vs. external value poking its head out again. In such a situation we would most likely look for things that possessed external worth to gather and sell. That's not the opportunity God saw; He used what was the most empty. Those empty vessels weren't half full with the world's water or system of wealth; they were empty enough to receive God's very best, and multiplication happened!

That's the opportunity I believe we have been given as we come alongside those who are battling poverty. Many of them the world would call empty vessels, but God sees their emptiness as open room in which they can receive the best of His promises already freely given. Each empty vessel has a purpose. If you notice in the story, the oil did not stop multiplying until there were no more empty vessels to receive it. Can you imagine if we empowered all the seemingly "empty vessels" around the world who are caught in their own poverty not just to receive, but to serve their greater purpose of redemption? In God's eyes, entering into their true purpose is greater than having escaped from their poverty. Maybe they aren't destined only to be rescued; just maybe, they are the ones God plans to use to change the world! It is this very possibility that we must continue to declare over each one from the very beginning: They are already seen and known by the Father as His child, with as much purpose as anyone. And in this way we will allow them to be freely filled with the oil of God, ready to flow out into other empty vessels.

Moving Forward:

1. Describe how we have turned poverty into an identity, and why this directly counters the mission of seeing poverty utterly obliterated from the earth.

2. Why do we need to see a revival of true identity within mission?

3. What is the potential of an "empty vessel"? What is the oil they need to receive?

Part 4: Addressing Physical Poverty

Just because we need to re-focus on the internal plagues of poverty and mistaken identity in mission, this does not mean we can't also fervently continue in supporting and giving abundantly to people's external needs at the very same time. But, we can tweak our motives and mindsets regarding how we give and how we address those battling poverty's unfriendly grip. And, since you are reading this book, you are already well aware that the Bible contains verses aplenty regarding our call to the poor. I'm not going to cite just one verse here because the Word of God itself is blooming with references to the promises that spring forth when we address those trapped in poverty. (You can probably even think of one or two of your own favorites.) Giving to alleviate poverty is the obvious part. The mindset behind such giving is where it gets murky.

I believe there is a ripe tension within our giving to the poor. This tension exists no matter where we are asked to give, whether to someone who is homeless in our own town, begging on the side of the road, or to someone on the streets of somewhere like Ethiopia or another third world nation where poverty's reach is vast in very real, and to be quite honest, sometimes manipulative ways. In fact, I'd say it is the encounters many of us have had with those who try to use poverty for their advantage that causes us to take a defined stance on how—and to whom—we give.

Poverty is very real, as you know. But it is also nastier than we realize, enslaving its victims without mercy. This is exactly why we are called to reveal Jesus through mercy and love, which bring freedom. Central to this area of giving to the poor is a question that often causes us to take sides. By our many guests and visitors in Ethiopia, we were frequently asked a specific question; we continued to learn its answer while walking the streets alongside them—an answer I'm still continuing to learn today. And the truth is that there is not one answer to live from, not one right filter to

155

process our giving through. There isn't a method dictating to whom you give or do not give among those begging on the streets. And now that I've discussed the answer (although not providing one!), maybe you want to know the question.

The question we face in our giving is whether our gift of the moment is being taken advantage of. Basically, we question whether the recipient is going to take our gift and use it for the wrong things or whether or not our gift will actually prove worthwhile. We don't want to be taken advantage of, nor in the process do we want to empower a negative in someone's life. Is that a question you have had? I know I have. And it's a question we were asked day after day while walking the streets with others in Ethiopia as those embarking upon mission pondered to whom they should or shouldn't give. The first time, giving can be a rush! The next time you start to recognize its muddy waters. And before you know it, you've crossed over to the other extreme.

The issue I have had to reconcile in my own fears of being taken advantage of by the vice of poverty in someone's life goes back to the nature of giving, and where it comes from. We give because it's what God calls for. We give because it is love. We give because Jesus gave in such a way, and we are called to be Jesus to the world. This is what I have had to reconcile: If I want to be Christ-like in my giving, then I must not only look at *what* Jesus gave, *or to whom*, but I must also look at *how* He gave. The greatest gift of all was Jesus stepping down into mankind's messy poverty of sin, the wages of which are death, and giving His life to redeem us from our poverty, all the while knowing not only that He and His gift could be taken advantage of, but that many would do so. He knew that many would choose not to receive the gift, and some would even use it for their own selfish desires and motives. *But He gave anyway*—and freely so! Jesus didn't measure the result when giving, He measured the moment, how the Father was moving Him, and thus how to reveal the Father to that individual through giving here on earth. Christ-like generosity is not measured by how it is received, but by how it is given. We can't try to be in control on both sides—that part isn't up to us. Once again, all we have to do is listen to His voice in our heart prompting us to give—then obey and entrust that person or those people to Him. If we are truly giving the way Jesus did, it means we will automatically place ourselves in position to be taken advantage of by people manipulating poverty, and therefore manipulating us. But that is the purpose of giving, to reveal the kindness and love of God. It is the kindness and love of God that leads us to repentance—before we deserve it (we never can deserve it!) and even before we are often ready to receive. Many times, there has to be a free, unwarranted gift, very likely to be abused, in order for an unconditional seed to be released into someone's life where it can freely, without our limitations, be nurtured by the Lord for the days and years to come. Often it is not *what* we give that truly makes a difference in someone's life, but *how* we give.

The other side of the story is one I have been on, too: when we are compelled by need and feel the only Godly thing is to give externally to *every* person who displays poverty. But that's not what Jesus did, either. My friend Caleb phrases it like this: "Just because we learn to stop for the one, doesn't mean we stop for every one." Jesus was not need driven, He was Father driven. He only joined the Father where He was moving, not everywhere some form of poverty was moving. It is as easy to align with this mindset as it is the one prior. Really, it is easier to align with any pre-defined stance on giving before we encounter each person rather than having eyes to see the Lord's unique and timely stance while interacting with each individual whom He loves and cherishes. The truth is, He is doing something different in each of them. Each need is very different, and only God knows the answer.

We must be willing to ask the Lord and find out His unique stance of love each and every time, with each individual. We are not just addressing poverty as a whole, but God uses us to address the whole through many parts. Each person has a different cycle, a different need, so a blanket answer from us only does so much. We have to be willing to not have a pat answer for poverty in order to help bring its true answer from, and with, the Lord. We have to be willing to walk poverty's streets without a prescribed "knowing" beforehand, instead being willing to learn each step of the way with Jesus. And the next day, we remember what we learned but avoid applying it just the same way, being careful not to recreate a method that is easy for us and others to subscribe to. We simply step out once again and make ourselves vulnerable like Jesus, clothed in His love and having our spiritual ears and eyes wide open to Him, willing to learn anew each day how to defeat poverty, *not according to our answer*, but with our living God leading us literally every step of the way.

Moving Forward:

1. Have you ever asked the question, "Am I being taken advantage of if I give to this person, or will my gift be used in the wrong way?" Talk about the experiences that have led to this question and how it has affected how you give.

2. What is the power offered through giving an unconditional gift? Though external appearances may show you otherwise, how can God use this unmeasured form of giving to impact a life?

3. Discuss what it looks like to avoid using a prescribed method of addressing poverty through giving. How might it look for you to join the Lord like that each step of the way?

CHAPTER 7:

CHANGING THE CULTURE OF MISSION

Part 1: One Step at a Time

We often have grand plans, and the Father loves for us to dream with Him in such ways, the key word being *with,* of course. But grand plans, realized promises and mission of lasting impact usually aren't accomplished in grand ways—at least not on our part, that is. As we've talked about now at great length, naturally we seem to want to go into something such as mission in one of two ways: We want to rush in according to our own noble, grandiose efforts, or we proceed only once we think we have a full understanding of how it will all come about. We like to have every track laid, every "I" dotted and all our ducks in a row. (Did I miss any clichés there?) But the reality is that God rarely works through our cultural clichés; instead, I believe He desires that we would rely far more on deep, unseen truths such as trust. Rather than waiting for us to have all our ducks in a row, I believe He is waiting for us to watch Him lay *His tracks* before us one step at a time, with us rarely able to see beyond our current step.

Such is a life of trust with Him, the very life of trust that originated in the Garden of Eden, and the very life of daily, one-step-at-a-time trust Jesus required of His followers. Why do we seem to think our culture is far enough advanced in maturity and understanding that we can skip that step and just live according to our "explanations" of mission rather than faithfully following God into the adventures He's planned for us? We too often fear surprises—the unknown—but it doesn't have to be that way if we know we are walking *with* Him. That's the thing. It sounds simple, but the basic revelation is that we're not doing mission for God, *but with Him.* To do mission *with* God places us right back on paths similar to those of so many of the heroes of faith we read about and are inspired by. The truth is, we can walk with Him the same way. But Moses wasn't on a mission to part the Red Sea, he was simply being led by God one step at a time. Abraham wasn't trying to be a pioneer exploring new, unknown territory, He was just listening to God and walking out those steps. Shadrach, Meshach and Abed-Nego certainly weren't looking for a fiery calling, but they stepped into one *with* Him. God is full of surprises that we can rarely see or comprehend at the outset of mission. But He is always there waiting to make His presence known along the way. Is there room for Him within our mission?

If we know what a good Father we have, then His surprises will by far surpass the assurances we usually want beforehand. This frees us up to live life and mission one step at a time, where some of His very best promises wait to be uncovered. When we think we can predict an outcome with God in mission, we probably have already limited Him. If we truly want to see biblical, God-sized results in mission, then greater trust beyond self is always part of the equation. Test this if you will. Look back over all those stories we marvel at in the Bible. How many of those people knew *what, how* or *when* God would answer? Did Daniel know how God planned to handle the lions? He stepped forward anyway. Did Peter know what the waves would feel like underfoot, or did he require a signed guarantee from Jesus before he took that first, simple step out of the boat? That's just it; they didn't have the answer, and they were okay with that because they stayed so intimate with God each step of the way, certain that He did have the answer and would show them at the opportune moment. These heroes of the faith didn't rush into their own mission trying to do something extravagant, nor did they wait for things to be explained before saying yes; they took one step at a time on the path of trust. This is often what we fear the most, yet it is also where God's best forms of mission are waiting to become testimonies of His crazy goodness to the world. Our fear, or lack of trust, keeps Him from being displayed more fully through our lives as the *real, good, living* God that He is.

> *"... as I was with Moses, so I will be with you.*
>
> *"You shall command the priests who bear the ark of the covenant, saying, 'When you have come to the edge of the water of the Jordan, you shall stand in the Jordan.'" So Joshua said to the children of Israel, "Come here, and hear the words of the Lord your God."*
>
> *"... It shall come to pass, as soon as the soles of the feet of the priests who bear the ark of the Lord, the Lord of all the earth, shall rest in the waters of the Jordan, that the waters of the Jordan shall be cut off. ..."*
>
> *Then the priests who bore the ark of the covenant of the Lord stood firm on dry ground in the midst of the Jordan; and all Israel crossed over on dry ground, until all the people had crossed completely over the Jordan. (Joshua 3:7-9, 13, 17)*

Something special, promised of God, was waiting for the Israelites on the other side of the Jordan—a *Promise Land,* in fact. God even assured Joshua that just as He had been with Moses, so would He be with Him. What's cool about this is that God didn't part the Jordan the same way He parted the Red Sea—similar outcomes, different methods. So what He wasn't saying is: "I'll do the same thing for you that I did for Moses." What He was saying was, *"I'll be with you to the same extent that I was with Moses."* God had surprise promises on the other side, and He promised to be present with the Israelites along the way. We can't have the promise on the other side without first engaging the promise of His presence on our way. The Israelites had to step through unknown circumstances to get to the other side, the same unknown we usually want to figure out before we move, and the waters of the Jordan were not parted until they had *already stepped into the water.* They had to step first, and then once more, and again, until they reached the other side. By the end, through their connection of trust with God, they had crossed the Jordan on dry ground, an impossible mission in the natural, but surprisingly possible when we're looking less for the answer and more at the One Who walks alongside us.

I believe crossing the Jordan is representative of our path and calling in mission. Something incredible awaits us on the other side, something much more than we can imagine, but we have to be willing to let go and take a step, not knowing ahead of time what God will do, only that it will be better than we could hope for. I love the exact words written in the passage above when it says that as soon as the feet of the priests "rest" in the waters, the waters will be cut off. That seems counter-intuitive to me. From the outside, it seems the word "rest" would be nowhere near an accurate description of such a daring step. That word alone is a reminder of what trust entails. Trust will move us forward with God faster than our feet can sprint through our own mission or agenda, but trust can't really be known, can it, unless we're resting in Him, having entrusted to Him our worries, cares, hopes and dreams? Just as you'd expect those priests to have had nervous, jittery feet while stepping into the waters *before* they were parted, those same places inside us must come to rest with God *before* we have exact answers spelled out, or already in our hands. Those answers don't need to be in our hands if they are already held in His, do they?

One of the defining mission moments in our family was a trip across Africa that became a seven-week trek across our own Jordan River. We had no pre-conceived answers, but God told us to step into the waters before they parted, and that only *then* we would walk through the river on dry ground. What did that look like? We were about to find out.

Destiny, our first-born daughter, Mercy (who had just turned four), and I were scheduled to visit seven nations all across different regions of Africa over a seven-week period. We would depart from Colorado in February for Rwanda, and travel home in April from South Africa. In between we were to hold meetings and conduct trainings in Ethiopia, Kenya, Botswana, Mauritius (a small island nation) and Madagascar. But here was our problem: We had our tickets to Rwanda, and we had tickets home from South Africa, nearly a continent apart from one another, but we didn't have funding for any of the flights in between. On top of that, we were told by a veteran of African mission and travels that for such an extensive trip we'd need at least $3,000 to cover basic expenses such as food, transport and lodging. We had only $500.

So, we went to the Lord to ask and listen. We felt Him speak fresh and clear to our hearts, *"Go, it's done. Step into the waters and you will walk through on dry ground."* You can imagine that our hearts didn't feel very "at rest," but we would learn. Each step of the way God provided miraculously, and each time the provision came in a completely different manner and just in time for our next step. God led us across the entire continent, including island areas, one step at a time. Each step, each flight, each hotel or guesthouse stay became quite the story of its own; all of which uniquely display just how good God is, and what we get to witness when we actually let go and allow Him that active "with" role in our lives and mission.

By the end of the trip, we hadn't been late for a single meeting, and we didn't miss one, either. If anything, God expanded our mission within the nooks and crannies of the trip that we might have ignored. We left with $500 for a family of three crossing Africa over seven weeks, gave away approximately half in the process, and still somehow came home with $250 in our pockets. I still don't understand that math, but I'm glad God does. I learned I didn't need to know how it all added up—only that He was able.

When we left our guesthouse in South Africa for home that April, Destiny, Mercy and I each picked up a rock, just as the Israelites had done as testimony after crossing the Jordan. We had walked through the river on dry ground, never knowing what the next step held, only that God was with us in the same way He had been with Moses and Joshua. Our job was to join Him, and trust Him, one step at a time.

In a culture in which we often want to rush into our grand ideas of mission, or wait until the waters part before we step, God often calls us to step into murky, intimidating, unknown waters with nothing more in our possession than trust. In my own life I've often referred to trust as "the feet to faith." I think of it this way because trust is the engine that actually empowers us forward in *God's* ways of mission. Trust is what allows us to keep stepping into the unknown. Mission is not a valiant, heroic attempt at crossing the Jordan, just as our goal was never to create a big, challenging trip across Africa. Our goal was to listen to God, step with Him, and trust Him with the rest. Simple trust says, *"I believe God is Who He says He is,"* and gives *Him* room to swoop in as the faithful hero and show the world just how good He is. Trust gives God room to move in our missions, as long as we move with Him.

Whether you're taking an adventurous trip across the unknowns of Africa, or simply stepping into one child's life, take those steps one at a time—*with God!* Don't rush, but don't be afraid to step into the unknown either. The Jordan River is a tension between the two. Trust enables us to live in that tension, and just wait until you see the promises He has in store on the other side—*and the power of His presence along the way*. They might seem a surprise now, but if you'll let Him walk you across that water, you just might realize God is more present and able in your life and mission than you ever really thought possible. Mission doesn't have to carry grandiose sex appeal or be overly planned out; it can be simple and surprising. The simple steps are up to us; the surprises we leave up to God.

Moving Forward:

1. Why do we let mission be dictated by so many of the cultural clichés and expectations of the world? What are the two ways we usually go into mission?

2. What does it mean in mission to step into the waters before they are parted? How might that look for you? If He is *with* you, is that just familiar Christian speech or is He really present?

3. Why is it important to let surprise be part of your walk with God? Can you trust Him with that?

Part 2: One Seed at a Time

"Do you not say, 'There are still four months and then comes the harvest?' Behold, I say to you, lift up your eyes and look at the fields, for they are already white for harvest!

"And he who reaps receives wages, and gathers fruit for eternal life, that both he who sows and he who reaps may rejoice together. For in this the saying is true: 'One sows and another reaps.' I sent you to reap that for which you have not labored; others have labored, and you have entered into their labors." (John 4:35-38)

Two perspectives in the previous passage stand out to me regarding Jesus' harvest: 1. Results are based on eternal life rather than being measured according to earthly standards. 2. We are either sowing or reaping, but we are rarely doing both. However, we typically form our mission from within the culture in which we live, and as much as our mission and harvest is supposed to be kingdom based, it tends to get muddied by culturally based perspectives and expectations. We live in a very results-oriented culture, which often, whether we know it or not, robs us of some of the kingdom possibilities within mission.

There is an unspoken need for our mission to be measured and then defined by results in order to prove its worth in a world of competing missions. I wish it weren't that way and I'm sure you agree. We shouldn't be using results or "numbers" to compete over funding. We shouldn't be competing at all. We should be partnering. But we rarely form our mission to partner with another; rather, whether intentionally or not, we form it to compete, or at least measure up so as to prove its worth through earthly results. How? In the previous verses, Jesus stated that some sow and others reap, that we may rejoice together. However, we rarely create mission focused just on sowing, letting everyone else know that we're expecting someone else to be reaping our results in nine months to a year. And rarely do we form our mission just to reap—while announcing that all this fruit we're now gathering is actually a result of what someone else has sown. See where we are going here?

We usually look at the model that's been elevated in front of us and build a mission designed both to sow and immediately reap. But is that really a healthy harvest? Is that the kind of harvest—or mission—to which we are called? What would happen if we changed the way we measured mission? Would it empower us to more freely and purely join the Lord where He is moving rather than being compelled to measure up to others? Mission isn't supposed to be measured according to earthly standards, but rather grown through multiplication. Yes, they will know us by our fruit, but the fruit Jesus spoke of in John 4 was eternal fruit, which isn't always readily seen by the naked eye. In fact, if we truly want to look at the fruit we are to measure by, the fruit of the Spirit the New Testament teaches us about is not a tangible, results-oriented fruit; rather it is an intangible assortment of things not easily measured, such as: love, joy, peace, patience, kindness, goodness and so on. The vast divide between the fruit we really should be producing and the poor substitute we often settle for causes me to grieve the ways we have allowed our culture to invade what we view as mission and how we construct those missions in the first place. Have we switched from the call to sow and reap for eternal benefits to a limited earthly approach that values towering fruit stacks over seeds sown? Is that then what leads us to seek identity in the amount of fruit we can measure rather than living *from* our identity as one who is already approved and chosen without need for such striving?

I have long had a picture in my head of someone tirelessly searching a barren, treeless land, climbing hills and braving tough conditions. Others are doing the same, and all have a heavy burlap bag on their backs that weighs on them and slows their journey. While thus burdened, they search for apples and fruit they may gather as their own. But fruit is hard to come by in this culture since it has already been picked clean. All the while, the harvesters do not realize that their heavy bags, which they consider such a burden, are nothing but a bag stocked with small, familiar, unplanted seeds! As they search the barren and needy land for fruit they can call their own, they have no idea that their bags carry the potential for hundreds upon thousands of trees that will not only bear fruit, but bear fruit for generations longer than anyone can measure or count. Rather than searching for fruit, these harvesters need to realize that they are sowers and that their "burdens" should actually be getting lighter with each step.

A seed can seem so little, insignificant and familiar. It takes new eyes, the eyes of faith, to see the tree waiting inside; let alone the abundant fruit that will grow from it naturally season after season. For a seed to burst and become this tree, it needs pressure. That is what our faith is for: We must apply the pressure of faith and timeless expectation every time God shows us the right soil in which to plant the seed, and then we trust, always knowing that love is an expert in sowing. Is our culture too far from a land where our mission might choose a seed over an apple? If apples can be found, your mission might look like you're doing well from the outset, but in choosing to plant seeds instead, you will be trusting God to make a barren land fruitful once again.

If we will see a renewal in our culture of mission I believe it must start with our valuing a seed culture in place of our results-oriented measurements. I believe it will require new eyes that already, by faith, value a seed for its eternal possibilities rather than looking at it as a waste of time without results. Are we willing to grow our mission by saying, "Yes, Lord, I'll join You in sowing, just please bring someone else to reap." Or, "Lord, thank you for showing me this ripe fruit, and thank you for those who years ago planted in faith what the world thought was only a simple seed."

I long to see missions that establish themselves as a seed culture and believe for multiplication rather than just simple addition of fruit. Our need to prove ourselves with apples goes down significantly once we have had our own internal poverty eliminated by the Lord's unconditional approval. The identity in mission we've spoken of at length goes a long way towards the foundation of a seed culture; a seed culture is birthed from identity. It's a culture of multiplication, where those who sow and those who reap come together to rejoice over one another's unique gifts and calling, and over the fields planted that they may not be able to label with their own logo or name, but fields that they know in the long run will produce a harvest that will transform countless lives and the entirety of the land. Are you merely after apples in mission, or will you listen to the still, small voice inside Who helps you to know where to plant a powerful seed?

Moving Forward:

1. Talk about the two roles of harvest in mission: sowing and reaping. How might things change if you only tried to focus on one at a time rather than both at once?

2. Why is it hard to value a seed over an apple? How do we let culture and our need for identity and worth impact which one we value more?

3. What is a seed culture and how might it impact the landscape of worldwide missions?

Part 3: Honor & Humility

"He must increase, but I must decrease." (John 3:30)

John the Baptist, who spoke those words, is one of my favorite examples of mission in the Bible because of how he prepared the way for Jesus, and therefore for all of us after Him. He is the epitome of both true humility and genuine honor. I believe John the Baptist, this great forerunner, paints a picture with his words and his life that will leave us seriously lacking if it is not embraced within our own forms of mission. Jesus Himself said of John that he was the greatest man ever born of woman (see Matthew 11:11), a prophet and so much more who not only saw differently, but wasn't afraid to live differently, either. One of our top goals in any mission should be to echo John's words with our life: *"He must increase, but I must decrease."*

Achieving this goal begins, of course, where all true mission first transpires—between the Lord and us. That is where John specifically directed his words, but a trickle-down effect involving our relationship to others naturally follows. One thing I have always found very important about those words of John the Baptist is the order in which he spoke them, an order I think we can tend to move slightly out of balance. It is no coincidence that John first talked about the need for the Lord to increase. That is our goal, for the Lord to increase in our lives and our mission—it must be less about our ways, more about Him and His. This is largely what we've talked about during this entire journey together as we have pointed to the importance of joining God where He is moving. It comes from an internal conviction that no mission I can do is enough by itself, no matter how good my intentions are. *I need more!* I need the Lord's presence and leading in my mission to increase to new levels. As soon as Jesus came on the scene, John was ready to surrender his mission and his ways to the new thing

God was ready to do. John the Baptist honored Jesus' ways of mission over his own and was ready to drop everything and join Him. Now *that* is honor!

John created room in his life and mission for Jesus to increase; this was priority number one and came before the point of decrease. That point is very important. Honor comes before humility because honor is what makes humility genuine. To give God increase automatically begins a healthy, natural progression of our decrease. But if we begin by trying to decrease, we operate in a false humility that is no different than pride itself, and that leaves us with little honor to give away. There is a fine line here, but an important one to grasp, so that the honor we give to another is genuine and able to multiply. Giving honor to someone creates a natural progression of humility that is essential as we learn to join the Lord in His mission. I've personally had my seasons where I got this right, and other seasons where I got this wrong. That is to say, a fear of pride will not elevate the Lord in our mission with the increase He's due. This kind of honor derives more from surrender than from lowliness we try to achieve on our own. Humility is not something we can strive for, it is something automatically birthed out of giving honor to another.

Like John, for us this process begins with the Lord as we let Him lead our ways of mission according to His best, fresh, timely ways. But it also spills over powerfully to those we interact with or minister to in mission. The more He increases in our lives and mission, the more He will increase in the lives of those we are privileged to touch. As much as we need to veer far away from that "hero" or "savior" mentality in mission, it is not any better if we strive unnaturally for the other extreme of our own self-mandated lowliness. Only that which is authentic gives birth, life and multiplication to true fruit. And as vital as it is that we go into mission with humility, I believe that posture begins with our ability to give genuine honor and increase to the Lord and others.

When we go onto the mission field, our goal is not to decrease in order to play a Christ-like role. Rather, we go into mission to empower others towards increase. We go in to meet and love on the broken right where they are, and give them the honor and increase that they may have never known before. We dive down to a lowly place not to be seen as humble servants; we dive down to a lowly place of washing their feet because our hearts burn to see them rise up with the Lord and be exactly who He sees them to be—a son or daughter of God flourishing in the midst of His family in their own special role. We dive down not because it is the direction we are trying to go, but because it is the place we are compelled to *lift them up from*. We dive down because we see, long before it is made manifest to physical eyes, the hidden honor and increase of the Lord in their lives that the world has squashed. Like John the Baptist, we must see Jesus shining within them waiting to come forth, leaving us desperate to abandon our "mission" and promote Christ in them. Honor precedes humility, but at the same time the two go hand-in-hand.

As we go out into whatever mission field the Lord has put before us, near or far, we will find opportunities to honor others instead of just ministering to them and their needs. We can honor their true identity instead of merely feeding their poverty. And sometimes, that honor might come differently than we first expect.

I remember visiting one of the poorest known communities in rural Ethiopia, a community that was stigmatized not only for poverty, but also for rampant drunkenness and prostitution— especially with girls of an extremely young an age. People from this tiny community struggled even to sell goods at the market because customers felt their items were marked with a scarlet letter of sorts. As you can imagine, this challenge in selling only increased their financial needs and forced even more to revert to heartbreaking means of survival. As entrenched in poverty's grip as they were during our visit, do you know what made the biggest difference that day? It wasn't anything we brought them to solve their poverty. It wasn't any "Americanized" gifts we could have bestowed. What blessed them most was the fact that we sat with them, that we embraced them, that we honored the true identity in which God sees them. We honored them not by speaking to them of how to get out of their current challenge, but by listening to them and their stories, by asking questions and valuing "who" they are. Again, rather than what we brought *to* them, they were honored by us receiving *from* them. Their blessing was to have some form, any form, of worth to give.

On that particular day it was their ability to use the little funds they had to buy us sodas. In typical means of "doing" mission, we almost require ourselves to be the giver. I mean, how can we take from someone who has so little, right? But as we have already discussed, sometimes receiving gives more than anything our hands could. Simply by saying yes to the drinks they put in our hands, we were able to honor an innate, human value in them that had been cursed by the world. Our ministry that day was simply to honor the value that they had a hard time seeing in themselves.

We tried to employ similar strategies of honor all throughout our time and mission in Ethiopia, and other nations as well. Honor is again one of those underrated, unseen forms of mission that promotes life in another, builds fruitful relationships and embraces a form of mission that John the Baptist himself employed in order to promote Christ. If we are going to truly promote Christ in our mission, it won't be accomplished by just speaking of Him or elevating Him over our lives; it will be accomplished by honoring Him within others. And when you see Him in another, you, too, will be compelled to dive low in order to give Him increase in their lives.

I love a simple, small quote from Rolland and Heidi Baker of Iris Ministries, based out of Mozambique. "Go low and slow," they always say. This is such a simple phrase to keep alive in our hearts for mission. Go low enough and slow enough wherever you are so that you can always recognize value that has been pushed down in others, to see where Christ is already alive and moving, and to take the time to recognize His mission in someone's life over your own ideas of mission. "Low and slow" helps us to honor God's ways of mission, as well as keeping us from missing out on giving Christ increase in the life of another. Isn't this what mission is all about, to promote Christ? If we are to give Him true increase, our mission doesn't need to increase, but the people we are touching do. Go low and slow, and see what the world might be missing, that which

Jesus Himself beckons our eyes to see.

Moving Forward:

1. Why is it important that we see the verse and calling from John the Baptist in the correct order?

2. Talk about what it might look like to employ a strategy of "honor" in mission.

3. What might it look like for you to go "low and slow?"

Part 4: Vision & Empowerment

This final section of the book I share with a full and heavy heart. Nothing has brought me more joy or heartache in mission than the subject of empowerment. It's a subject that has been interwoven and mentioned all throughout this journey, but I want us to end by looking at it together with a more focused emphasis.

I believe empowerment goes beyond what we usually make of discipleship. Empowerment is what Jesus did by going away, sending the Spirit, transforming His closest followers from disciples into apostles who themselves became transformers of culture. But, wow, can empowerment be messy! Often in the same vein, we want to be empowered but we are also scared of being empowered, because it requires a measure of personal responsibility calling one to step up, and step out. Empowerment is imperative, though, if we want to leave any and every form of poverty behind because it is the opposite of what keeps us bound in cycles of dependence—whether spiritual, physical or emotional in nature.

We've had our fair share of dealings with each of these different cycles, and we have learned a lot. Empowerment is not for the faint of heart, as it requires us to live by trust and the unseen rather than allowing us to be in control or see immediate results. Empowerment is what we do with the seed we plant; we recognize its potential, prepare it, help it find ripe soil and then let go and trust that seed to God. And like digging in the soil, empowerment can be messy. It involves forward movement, which requires new, unknown steps, brings dreaded change and, therefore, demands our trust. There is that "trust" word again. This explains why we don't follow through so often—because we don't want to give up control. To truly empower someone, however, we can't dictate the results. We can't prove our reasoning for releasing that seed into ripe soil. We can't control peoples' obedience or what they ultimately do with that seed. Nor can we bring everyone into our mind to understand our own efforts to obey God.

During our time in Addis Ababa we worked with a group of kids from the streets into whom we had poured more than a year of time, love, teaching and resources. Everything had been built around empowering them, and they were truly "getting it." They were learning to go to God as their Source, and they were seeing miracles of provision happen in their lives—direct and timely answers to prayer. They were growing deeper with the Lord and they were going out and impacting others. The first stages of empowerment still require your presence, discipleship and varied forms of dependence, just like a child before being released into college or the "real world." This dependence isn't wrong; *it is necessary.* But it also must be leading them forward towards a bigger vision for their lives, with the goal of empowering them to walk into such. Eventually, that was the issue we ran into with this particular group of kids. They liked the idea of empowerment, but they had run poverty's race around that track so many times that they were still very comfortable not transitioning out of dependence. Truly, they were in a war with themselves. They wanted to be empowered, but they also wanted to stay comfortable and hold onto the only life they knew, even if that life was a cycle of poverty.

These kids weren't alone in their battle—they had many people with dear intentions showing them the love of God, but without a vision to accompany such love—a role I have played many times, by the way. I believe we have to give those in poverty apples, but we must do so while giving them vision for the hidden seed inside at the same time. I'm not pointing the finger; I've given out plenty of apples without offering the vision or purpose of the seeds. But we continued to watch the cycle of dependence pull these boys, into whom we had poured so much, back into its grasp as they were still being fed incessantly by foreigners in the touristy area of town. They didn't need to keep stepping forward out of poverty when they realized enough people would shower them with gifts right where they sat. This caused all the change we had been watching in their hearts start to unravel before our eyes. For every step forward they took towards long-term change, at the same time, perhaps just later in the day, they would find someone willing only to feed their poverty. This left the boys with a crisis of decision: Do we want change or do we want to remain comfortable? The tough responsibility I knew that I carried was to love them deeply, while also showing them they had to keep walking forward with us. We would continue to feed them, we would continue to teach them, help them find jobs, anything we could. We loved those boys! And most of all, we were still willing to walk side-by-side with them as long as they, too, were walking forward, rather than remaining in their comfortable and familiar circles of poverty. But they found too many willing to feed old ways. As a result, they couldn't break out. And please hear me on this as I say it with a heavy heart: I am not blaming the people who fed the poverty in those boys. Nor am I blaming the boys. What I am saying is that empowerment is hard, very hard; but it is also necessary if we will see every person who battles poverty have the opportunity to be who God made them to be. We currently have a lack of vision within mission to see empowerment through to its fulfillment. That is what must be changed.

We were left with an excruciating decision sure to leave us either aiding something we were trying to see broken, or appearing insensitive because from all outer appearances we would be "abandoning" these precious kids. We could allow the boys to keep playing both sides, even reverting back to games and manipulation with us, or tell them we love them, that we'll always be there if they change their mind, ready to walk forward with them once more. We chose the latter. Why? Because if we truly wanted to see their poverty destroyed and see each of those boys flourish, then we could not feed the enemy of poverty that they were welcoming back in each day. But see, this is what happens all over the planet. This is why identity, empowerment and true vision must be revived in mission, starting with us, and be reproduced in others. If we don't join together to change our perspective—our vision—in mission, and help those in poverty walk forward, feeding them along the way, then we are only going to spin our wheels in mission and continue to re-enforce different sides of the cycle—unknowingly warring against one another and planting on grounds where we have disabled the ability for growth.

The person trying to walk out of poverty's grip does not have to display perfection; there only has to be a willing heart and a desire to keep stepping forward out of comfortable cycles. Our goal can no longer rest at such a short finish line as feeding bellies—even as vitally important and non-negotiable as that is. We have to go further from the outset, beginning from step one. We have to see the vision for their lives that Jesus sees, beyond the tattered externals that we see. We must choose from the get-go a destination that is nothing short of seeing that person walking in his or her true identity as a son or daughter of God, with which comes salvation, all the while feeding him or her physically, spiritually, mentally and emotionally along the way.

The issue is not about our actions, but the vision we are using and giving. There is a poverty of vision within mission, and precious kids are slipping further into true poverty as a result. We need to lift our eyes up higher to see. If we sell our vision short, we teach others to sell their vision short. We reproduce what we live. If we are living without vision and identity, so will those we reach in missions—and the cycle will continue. But if we all live by fresh, uniquely given vision with the Lord, we will reproduce the same, and before we know it we will see those in poverty not only escape their old cycles but begin to run the race of purpose, becoming champions in our world. *Their purpose is greater than their poverty.* Aim them towards their purpose, and you'll see the answer to their physical poverty added in; aim just to alleviate their physical poverty, and in the long run, they will neither enter their true purpose nor escape their poverty.

Vision is the key to empowerment. As we highlighted in Chapter 5, *"where there is no vision, the people perish" (Proverbs 29:18, KJV)*. Ever since returning from Ethiopia as we have traveled to speak on mission, we are always asked how we defeat poverty. And once again, it is an inside out answer rather than outside in. We firmly believe—as we have learned firsthand, both the hard way and the joyous way—that vision, and all its partners in mission, is the answer to poverty. Now, vision is very multifaceted, so that isn't just one answer in itself. In fact, it's the possibility of many answers. It is empowering each person to see the change that's possible not only in their lives, but in the world. Vision provides hope. Hope matures into faith. Faith births passion, and passion reveals purpose. Ultimately, vision helps change the root question in a person's heart from poverty's refrain of, "How am I going to survive?" to a question without limits that asks, "Who am I and what have I been created for?" Very simply, to give someone vision is to change the foundational perspective they live from, allowing them to shatter the strongholds that have tried to strangle them and replacing these lies with God's perspective placed directly before the eyes of *their* heart. Helping someone to achieve personal vision through God's lens is one of the greatest ways we can empower him or her. A great Christian teacher, Dan Mohler, says this succinctly: "If you can change a man's perspective, you can change his whole life."[1]

My stomach churns just writing this because it is such a touchy subject; it isn't understood by mere external views. We all have to dig deeper, and that goes much further than any book can share. I want your heart to want His perspective and nothing less! What I can do is paint a picture of possibility, of purpose, of perspective largely untapped, of lives changed through empowerment, and of many who still wait to be changed. I hope you remember these lives and stories of transformation that have been shared in this journey, and I pray you understand the many more just like this last group of boys who haven't been able to grasp empowerment's opportunity—yet! They are the majority. They are the ones who wait for those like us to live mission from the Father's perspective rather than from the view *we* are comfortable with. As we join together in pursuit of new vision and empowerment in mission, I believe all such as these will have that opportunity.

I hope in this journey together you have seen a glimpse of the Father's perspective and have become excited about what still remains possible around the world. There is a revival waiting to happen once we discover our true identity in mission! I pray you see poverty differently now, for the insidious monster it really is— underhandedly playing us against one another to retain its grip on those without vision and knowledge of their true identity.

I ask that you seek God for His vision. Don't just take my word for it—He'll show you for yourself if you ask Him. There is a lot He'll show you if you go straight to the Source. He'll show you mission, He'll show you purpose, He'll reveal true identity and multiply it even further out of you towards others. He will teach you if you will let Him. That is my request. Don't do mission with me, or my way, do mission *with Him*. Become an echo of Christ's own words that say, ***"The Son can do nothing of Himself, but what He sees the Father do; for whatever He does, the Son also does in a like manner" (John 5:19).*** Don't rely on the world, Christian culture, this book or status quo for vision. Choose to go straight to the Source and let all mission flow from there. Choose to see differently. Choose to see whom God is waiting to empower around the world. Choose to let your life and mission be a reflection of what is seen through Love's eyes.

Moving Forward:

1. Describe the potential power and the real pain that can be present with empowerment.

2. In what ways do we unknowingly spin the wheels of poverty? How will vision break that cycle?

3. Summarize what it means, or could mean, to live mission through God's eyes.

End Notes:

1. Revival Lifestyle [@RevivalQuotes]. 10 May 2013. "If you can change a man's perspective, you can change his whole life." – Dan Mohler [Tweet]. Retrieved from https://twitter.com/Dan_Mohler.

ABOUT THE AUTHOR

Joey and his wife, Destiny, live in Castle Rock, Colorado with their five children. Joey is a visionary at heart, a passionate speaker, and the author of six books. Together, Joey and Destiny travel extensively with a heart for the nations and a vision to empower each person into their own unique purpose and calling. They have founded Imagi-Nations LLC, which empowers at-risk youth around the world to live their purpose and dream.

For contact or to book a training, please e-mail:
joey.letourneau@gmail.com

Find more of Joey's books, or learn about "Imagi-Nations LLC" at www.uncommonvision.org or joeyletourneau.com.

Made in the USA
Lexington, KY
01 July 2014